$2
6/21

Can I Freeze It?

Can I Freeze It?

How to Use the Most Versatile Appliance in Your Kitchen

Susie Theodorou

Photography by Deirdre Rooney

WM
WILLIAM MORROW
An Imprint of HarperCollins Publishers

A hardcover edition of this book was published in 2007
by William Morrow, an imprint of HarperCollins Publishers.

CAN I FREEZE IT? Copyright © 2007 by Susie Theodorou.
Photographs copyright © by Deirdre Rooney.

HarperCollins books may be purchased for educational, business, or sales
promotional use. For information please write: Special Markets Department,
HarperCollins Publishers, 10 East 53rd Street, New York, NY 10022.

First paperback edition published 2009.

Designed by Level, Calistoga, CA
Recipe testing and assistant food stylist, Beth Pilar

The Library of Congress has cataloged the original hardcover edition as follows:

Theodorou, Susie.
   Can I freeze it?: how to use the most versatile appliance in your kitchen /
Susie Theodorou.—1st ed.
      p. cm.
   ISBN: 978-0-06-079702-7
   ISBN-10: 0-06-079702-9
   1. Frozen foods.   2. Make-ahead cookery.
   TX610.T42 2007
   641.6'153—dc22

                                                                    2006047498

   ISBN 978-0-06-180246-1 (pbk.)
   09   10   11   12   13   QXD/TP   10   9   8   7   6   5   4   3   2   1

To my mother, grandmothers, and aunts—all wonderful cooks

contents

acknowledgments

A cookbook, no matter how big or small, cannot be done without the help of friends and colleagues—especially when one is a freelancer.

The biggest thank you must go to Beth Pilar and Deirdre Rooney. Beth, for her patience and care in testing many of the recipes and for her honest comments. Deirdre, for her guidance in art direction and beautiful photographs for this book. I remember it was so, so hot during the shoots, but Deirdre and Beth worked super-hard and with humor—there was no air-conditioning in the studio! It was fun, but not always easy.

To Frigidaire, for the loan of a smart standup, frost-free freezer that was a great help during the writing, testing, and photographing of the recipes for this book.

To Staub USA Inc. and Le Creuset of America Inc. for the use of their beautiful pots, co-cottes, roasting dishes, wok, and grill pan used for testing the recipes and in some of the photographs—thank you.

A big thank you to Jean Conlon, Clive Streeter, and Valerie Berry for the loan of their studios for the shoots.

To my dear art-director friends, Matthew Axe and Scot Schy, who offered me sound advice during the shoots. They listened to me on short notice—most appreciated. Thank you.

Thank you so much to my family of friends in New York who put up with the dinner parties in my non-air-conditioned apartment, where shamelessly I pushed my recipes on them. All your comments were taken on board.

To Jane Druker, Bill Tikos, and Liz Marcy for helping me get this book off the ground, into a project, and finally a book. Thank you.

To Level for their design—I am very happy our paths have crossed.

And finally, thank you to Harriet Bell for believing in this idea, and to everyone at Harper-Collins who has guided me through the stages of producing a book.

introduction

In many homes, the freezer is nothing more than a place to display family photos and children's artwork, attached with a collection of magnets. Or, worse still, the freezer can be a dusty repository in the basement or garage to which too-good-to-pass-up supermarket bargains are consigned, never to be used.

Can I Freeze It? will help you transform your freezer into the most essential appliance in your kitchen, allowing you to prepare family meals as well as dishes for entertaining well ahead of time. If the cupboard is bare, at least the freezer will be full of make-ahead meals, sweet and savory frozen pies, and other dishes.

"Can I freeze it?" is the question I'm most often asked when giving out recipes. This book explains what you can and can't freeze successfully and offers lots of recipes that show how to use your freezer to its best advantage. On the other hand, this isn't an encyclopedic guide to preparing and freezing seasonal fruits and vegetables from the garden or farmers' market. You will find information on how to make the most of your freezer space, how to freeze foods effectively, and most of all how to prepare dishes for the freezer without it becoming a chore.

perfect freezing

every time

Freezer Basket

how freezing works

Freezing preserves food by slowing down the growth of the microorganisms that cause decay. It does not kill microorganisms; but to grow they require water, and if the water within the cells of the food has been turned into ice, that means it is unavailable for bacterial growth and chemical reactions.

In order to achieve proper freezing and prevention of decay, a constant temperature of 0°F/–18°C or less is required. Some freezers cannot achieve or are not kept at that temperature. If the temperature in the freezer fluctuates, the length of time foods can be kept is reduced considerably. In order to help maintain the lowest possible temperature, keep freezer doors closed as much as possible, add small quantities of unfrozen food at a time, and make sure that all prepared food has cooled to room temperature before it is placed in the freezer.

The faster food is frozen, the better, as fast freezing creates smaller ice crystals. Food that is frozen slowly develops large ice crystals that can pierce the cell walls, possibly causing a compromise in the flavor and texture of many foods.

Always place unfrozen food in the coldest part of the freezer until solid, then organize the freezer as appropriate, with foods that are to be stored the longest kept in the coldest parts at the back, and foods that will be used quickly kept close to the front or on top.

Many freezers have a "fast-freeze" switch, which lowers the temperature to enable food to be frozen more quickly. Once the food is solid, turn off the fast-freeze switch. Other models have a thermostat dial so you can turn the dial to its lowest temperature setting while the food is freezing and then once the food is frozen solid, return the dial to the original setting. Don't forget to do so, as these dials may also control the temperature within the refrigerator.

Last, a word on what happens when freezing goes wrong. The telltale sign of freezer burn is a frosty, gray appearance on the surface of the food; freezer burn can cause the prepared food to taste spoiled and tough. This happens when air dries out the surface of the food as it is in the freezer. It can easily be prevented by wrapping the foods tightly with the correct materials.

freezing tips and techniques

When freezing food, make sure you leave plenty of clear space around each container or package you are freezing to allow the air to flow around the unfrozen food and freeze the food quickly and evenly. After the packages are frozen, stack them more efficiently.

Foods frozen in smaller quantities will freeze faster than foods frozen in larger quantities, helping to prevent a buildup of large ice crystals.

Use shallow containers with a wide surface area relative to depth. This will enable food to freeze quickly all the way through. If using plastic freezer bags for meats, vegetables,

sauces, or soups, seal them well, then place them flat on a chilled baking sheet until frozen solid. Again, a wide surface area will aid in the formation of tiny ice crystals and will also make for faster thawing.

It is important to cool food completely to room temperature before freezing. Placing hot foods in the freezer will raise its temperature, slowing down the freezing time and possibly thawing other foods, and the centers of the foods may not freeze quickly enough to prevent spoilage.

To make sure that foods such as uncooked meatballs, ground meat patties, dumplings, ravioli, cookies, profiteroles, meringues, and individual cakes retain their shapes and remain separate upon freezing, use the open-freeze or dry-freeze method to freeze food quickly on all sides. Place a baking sheet lined with parchment paper or plastic wrap in the freezer and chill for 10 to 20 minutes. Place the food in a single layer on the lined baking sheet, leaving about 1 inch between the pieces, and freeze for about 1 hour or until solid. Then pack in plastic freezer bags, vacuum-sealed bags, or airtight freezer-safe plastic containers and return to the freezer. Be sure to mark the packages or containers with their contents and the date.

containers

Choose packaging materials that will protect the food's flavor, color, moisture content, and nutritional value from the dry climate of the freezer. Containers should:

❊ **Not become brittle and crack at low temperatures. Look for the freezer symbol, often a snowflake, to indicate that it is freezer safe.**

❊ **Be durable, leakproof, and easy to seal and mark.**

❊ **Be oil, grease, and water resistant (no uncoated paper containers).**

❊ **Protect against absorption of outside flavors and odors.**

Glass and Ceramic: If using glass containers, choose dual-purpose types that are designed for freezing and also are heat-proof. Pyrex and Simax are brands made from boro silicate glass, which cannot go from freezer to hot oven immediately—the dish must stand at room temperature for at least 3o minutes, as the sudden heat change may cause it to break. Dishes with tempered glass such as Anchor Hocking and Duralex must be completely thawed before placing in a hot oven. If you're using glass jars to freeze sauces, soups, or stocks, be sure to leave at least a $\frac{3}{4}$- to 1-inch space at the top, as the water in the recipe will expand and may cause the glass to break if filled too high.

There are also many brands of freezer-to-oven-to-table ceramic dishes, such as CorningWare. These are especially good for baked pastas and casseroles, as they can be placed in the oven straight from the freezer, and then brought to the table. Be sure they are suitable for freezer use.

Plastic: Make sure the containers close tightly and securely and are made of plastic that will not become brittle at a low temperature; look for the snowflake symbol on brands such as Sistema, Klip It, or Lock & Lock. All three have a clipping system for closing the top. Plastic containers are good for foods that have been frozen with the open-freeze or dry-freeze method, as they protect more fragile items, such as meringues, profiteroles, and pastries, from being damaged or crumbled by other bags and containers of food. They also allow you to take out and use as much food as required, resealing the remainder in the plastic container for another day.

Plastic Freezer Bags: Be sure to use only plastic bags that are labeled for freezer use. Once the bag is filled, try to squeeze out as much air as possible in order to prevent ice crystals from forming around the food in the bag. Once the air is squeezed out, tightly close the bag, either by sealing with the attached zipper lock, or by twisting the top of the bag and fastening tightly with a freezer clip or plastic-coated wire twist-tie. Bags are best used for small to medium quantities; it's faster to thaw two smaller bags than it is one large one. When using freezer bags, ideally freeze flat until solid, then store upright or stack with other frozen foods. Food that is frozen flat will thaw much more quickly than food that is frozen in one big lump.

Vacuum-Sealed Bags: These excellent bags work by sucking the air out of the filled bag and heat sealing it at the same time, thus completely eliminating the possibility of freezer burn and flavor deterioration. While this method is optimal, you will have to buy the vacuum-sealing machine and the special bags. Items such as burgers, meatballs, and fishcakes must be frozen solid first (by the open-freeze or dry-freeze method) or they will become misshapen when the bag is sealed. Meat stews need to be completely cold with their juices well jelled together; otherwise the moisture will be drawn out and clog the machine, as well as prevent a successful seal to the bag. The vacuum seal is also good for sealing cuts of raw meat,

chicken, and fish. The drawback to this system is that once the bag is opened, you either must thaw all the food inside or reseal the portion you are not using immediately.

Plastic Wraps and Aluminum Foil: Good materials for wrapping meats and other large or irregularly shaped foods include freezer-coated paper, plastic wrap, and heavy-duty aluminum foil. You'll notice that freezer paper is shiny on one side; place food directly on the shiny side. Waxed paper can be used to keep food separate in freezer-safe containers. Freezer-safe plastic wrap allows for a super-tight wrap. For extra safe-keeping, after being wrapped in plastic freezer wrap, food should then additionally be wrapped in either heavy-duty foil or placed in a plastic freezer bag. Do not use regular plastic wrap, which is porous and can lose its clinging qualities under sustained cold temperatures, possibly allowing foreign odors to penetrate the food. Also refrain from using regular-weight foil, as it becomes brittle at low temperatures. Avoid parchment and greaseproof paper, which becomes soggy on freezing.

organizing the freezer

Freezers should be kept at 0°F/−18°C. If your freezer or fridge-freezer does not show the exact temperature digitally, consider keeping a refrigerator/freezer thermometer in the freezer. If the temperature rises above 0°F/−18°C, turn down the dial in the refrigerator/freezer to lower the temperature.

Look for stars on the freezer compartments. The stars indicate the temperature of the compartment and how long food may safely be stored there.

❋ One star (21°F/−6°C) is fine for making ice cubes and is sufficiently cold to keep food for three or four days.

❋ Two stars (10°F/−12°C) stores food for fifteen to twenty days.

❋ Three stars (0°F/−18°C) will keep food safe for up to three months.

❋ Four stars (below 0°F/−18°C) means that the compartment provides the ideal conditions for freezing fresh and precooked foods.

Once food is placed in appropriate freezer storage containers, try to avoid throwing it in the freezer at random. It is well worth making the time to package, date, and label food and to place it so that you can see right through to the back or bottom of the freezer. If the freezer is deep, keep a list on the door that itemizes the contents. Use a nonmetal rack to create shelves (see photograph on page 13), so that everything is not simply piled up on top of everything else and so that you can access items more easily.

For maximum efficiency, keep your freezer at least 75 percent full; otherwise you'll lose the cold air each time the freezer is opened.

maintaining the freezer

Although manual-defrosting freezers are rarely manufactured because they are not as energy efficient as frost-free freezers, many people still own them. They should be defrosted at least twice a year or when there is more than ¼ inch of frost inside. Accumulated freezer frost reduces storage space and energy efficiency. Schedule the big clean when the food inventory is low so that the process can be completed as quickly as possible—within, say, a couple of hours.

To clean the freezer, first remove all food and pack it in coolers with ice packs or in cardboard boxes with layers of newspaper to prevent the food from thawing. Put in a cool place. Disconnect the freezer from the electrical supply and place a pan and towels in the bottom of the freezer to catch any water and a bowl near the draining tube just outside the freezer to catch excess water. As models differ from one another, consult the manufacturer's instructions for thawing. Some recommend placing a bowl or tray of hot water inside the freezer to quicken the process; others may recommend just using a fan. Once the ice starts to loosen, use a wooden or plastic spatula to ease it gently away from the freezing elements. When all the frost has been removed, sponge the interior with a cleaning solution of either 1 to 2 tablespoons baking soda per 1 quart water or 1 cup white vinegar per 1 gallon water. Rinse with clean water and dry with an absorbent cloth. Make sure the freezer is completely cooled down before switching it back on, then close the door and allow it to run for 15 to 20 minutes before returning the food to the freezer.

Frost-free freezers obviously require no defrosting, but they do need to be cleaned out at least twice a year to discard any expired food. To clean the freezer, follow the procedure as above, storing frozen food in coolers or cardboard boxes, wiping the interior clean with a baking soda or vinegar solution, rinsing and toweling dry, and then bring to freezing temperatures before replacing the food.

thawing

Freezing to 0°F/−18°C inactivates but does not destroy the microbes—bacteria, yeasts, and molds—present in food. Once thawed, these microbes can again become active, multiplying under the right conditions to levels that can lead to food poisoning.

There are three safe ways to defrost food: in the refrigerator; immersed in a bowl of cold water; or in the microwave.

Refrigerator: Thawing food in the refrigerator is the safest method. Perishable foods (meat, poultry, fish/seafood, and dairy) and precooked foods high in moisture content should be thawed in the refrigerator. The temperature must remain at 40°F/4°C or lower. Food thawed in the refrigerator will then keep in the refrigerator for up to three days once completely thawed.

The rules for safe refrigerator thawing are:

* Place the bag or container on a rack over a tray or plate to catch any drips

* Always keep the frozen food in its wrapping or new wrapping if necessary

* Thaw foods on a shelf below ready-to-eat food

Plan well ahead for this method, as you will need to allow about:

* 8 hours per pound of meat

* 4 hours per pound of poultry

* 6 hours per pound of fruit and vegetables

* 12 to 24 hours for stews and casseroles

Some foods actually benefit from slow thawing. The meats for stir-fries and for grilling, broiling, and roasting become more tender and more flavorful thanks to the slow defrosting/marinating process. Beef and chicken stews develop, deepen, and mellow in flavor as they defrost, the slower, the better. Many recipes have been developed with a larger quantity of sauce than usual to keep the meats well coated and protected from drying out during freezing.

Bowl of Cold Water: This is often called the fast thawing method. Use this method for soups, sauces, marinating meats, poultry, or fish, and cubed meat stews.

❋ Place frozen food in a watertight, sealed bag

❋ Keep quantities small, such as two chops or chicken breasts or 1 pint of tomato sauce per bag

❋ Place in a large bowl and completely immerse in cold water, not below 70°F/21°C

❋ Change the water every 30 minutes

❋ Do not continue this process for more than 2 hours

❋ Never use hot water

An alternative method would be to have cold running water from the tap pouring onto the food, following the rules above.

Microwave: The microwave is the most efficient method of thawing foods. The microwave process actually starts the cooking of food, hence the importance of thorough cooking immediately afterward. Important points to remember:

❋ Use the microwave method for small amounts of food only

❋ Make sure foods are wrapped in microwave-safe plastic wrap or containers, never foil

❋ Allow 6 to 8 minutes per pound of food when thawing in the microwave on low heat or defrost

❋ Once the food is thawed, reheat on high, or remove from the microwave and cook as required by a conventional stove, oven, broiler, or grill

Exceptions to the Rule: Precooked foods low in moisture content (breads, cakes, and cookies) can be thawed at room temperature. Unwrap the cake or cookies, place on a cooling rack, and allow to thaw for 30 to 60 minutes. Breads should be covered loosely to prevent drying out, for 2 to 3 hours at room temperature. You can toast waffles, bagels, and sliced bread straight from the freezer.

how to choose
the right freezer

There is a huge range of freezers to choose from, including different shapes and sizes to suit the needs of every household. Consider the number of people in your home, whether you'll be freezing large quantities of fresh produce or meat (if you plan to buy fresh food in bulk and freeze for later in the week or month), how much floor space you have available, what energy efficiency and de-frosting features you prefer, and whether you are willing to pay for extra bells and whistles on high-end models.

There are four types of freezers on the market:

1. Refrigerator-Freezer Combination

This is a single appliance with one or two doors. It has one compartment for frozen foods and another for refrigerated foods. The freezing compartments may be above, below, or to one side of the refrigerated area. If select-ing this type, be certain that the freezer is a true freezer (able to maintain 0°F/-18C or less) and not just an icebox. Some refrigerators feature a small icebox that opens within the refrigera-tor itself. It is important to note that this is sufficient only for making ice cubes or storing ice cream and maybe a bag of frozen peas—it cannot be considered a true freezer.

Models that feature the freezer on top are usually the most inexpensive fridge/freezer combinations to purchase and are more space efficient than comparably sized side-by-side models. Widths can range from 30 to 33 inches, and there are often two levels—if not, it is well worth adding a rack stand of your own.

These freezers are conveniently at eye level and are therefore easy to access; the shallow depth allows you to see to the back. Another advantage to this style of freezer is that a high proportion of its actual size, usually around 80 percent, is useable freezer capacity.

Models that feature the freezer below are often from the designer range of fridge/freezer brands. They open either with a pull-out drawer-style door or a conventional door and feature another drawer inside to give two levels of storage. The widths typically range from 30 to 36 inches but the proportion that is actual freezer space is lessened due to the way the pull-out drawers work, though this is still typically more space than is offered by the side-by-side type of freezer.

Side-by-side models feature freezer and fridge right next to each other, with the freezer typically half the width of the fridge. The combined width is typically 32 to 48 inches. These freezers are deep relative to their width, which can make accommodating large, wide objects, such as turkeys, difficult. It can sometimes be hard to find food hidden at the back, too. But there is often plenty of storage on the freezer door, and most models of this type come equipped with a through-the-door water dispenser. These side-by-side models typically offer the least usable freezer space in relation to their size when compared to the two other fridge/freezer models.

2. Upright Freezers

These appliances have the same general shape and appearance as home refrigerators. They have one or two outside doors and from three to seven shelves or pull-out bins for storing food. Freezers of this type are popular due to their convenience, the small floor space they require, and the ease with which food may be put in or removed. However, large amounts of cold air escape each time the door is opened, which can diminish their efficiency.

3. Chest Freezers

Chest freezers are wide, deep freezers that open from the top with a hinged lid. Often, they're kept in a garage or a room separate from the kitchen, as they require a great deal of floor space. These types of freezers can be very useful if you have a large household, live a long way from where you buy your food, or have a large garden that yields lots of produce for home freezing. They are the most efficient in terms of capacity and are also best at keeping food frozen on a long-term basis. They're also relatively inexpensive to purchase, but their biggest drawback is the fact that it's difficult to keep track of what you have in there because of the way that the food is piled up on top of itself. They normally come with two interior baskets, but these generally aren't sufficient to create an organized space. Using plastic crates is a good way of separating foods within the freezer and keeping track of what's at the bottom—make sure you purchase crates that won't be brittle at low temperatures, and select thick, industrial-looking crates rather than thin-walled store-cupboard-style crates.

4. Integrated Freezers

These are the absolute latest in freezer design. The freezer is integrated into the kitchen cabinets, most often just below the counter, in the form of a drawer or a series of drawers—whatever you might want. Each drawer has a depth of 24 inches and a height of 19½ inches. You can have a built-in ice-maker as well. With these, you can pull out the whole drawer—no secrets in the back or bottom of the freezer. They also come combined with a refrigerator drawer above the freezer drawer.

What Does Frost Free Mean?

The latest important innovation in refrigeration is frost free technology, which saves hours of chipping away at thick layers of ice when the door won't close anymore! In a frost-free freezer, every six hours or so a timer turns on a heating device, which is wrapped among the freezer coils. The heater melts the ice off the coils. When all the ice is gone, a temperature sensor senses the temperature rising above 32°F/0°C and turns off the heater. This is why frost-free freezers have glass shelves and baskets and no signs of metal bars or electrical elements. Upright freezers and fridge/freezers are available as manual-defrost or frost-free models, whereas chest freezers are only available as manual-defrost.

As beautiful, clean, and convenient as frost-free freezers are, it is important to know that heating the coils every six hours takes energy and cycles the food in the freezer through temperature changes. For this reason, manual-defrost freezers keep food safe longer and are more energy efficient, provided they are kept ice free by regular manual defrosting.

Where to Put Your Freezer

Whatever type of freezer you select, it should be placed in a cool, dry, and well-ventilated place; never by a stove or a water heater or in the sun, as this makes it more difficult to maintain a temperature of 0°F/−18°C or lower. Do not push the freezer flush against a wall, as it needs about 2 inches of space for air circulation. And be sure the freezer sits level; if left unleveled for a long period of time, the body of the freezer can become so deformed that the door will not close properly. Also, if the freezer does not sit straight, it may cause leakage and the motor may sound louder than usual.

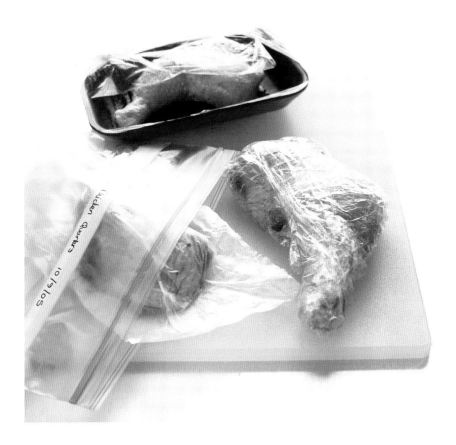

foods that freeze well

Your freezer really can be used as a bonus bag of groceries. Consider which staples and basic ingredients you could freeze to use along with fresh ingredients in your cooking. In my opinion, no freezer should be without frozen peas, corn kernels, spinach, dumplings, ravioli, fresh pasta noodles, and meat, chicken, or vegetable stock.

For long-term freezing of **fresh meat** (i.e., for more than one week), be sure to remove it from its plastic supermarket packaging (unless your butcher has wrapped your purchases specifically for freezer storage). This plastic wrapping is actually designed to allow oxygen in to keep the color of the meat bright, and while this is fine for refrigerated storage, it leads to freezer burn in frozen storage. Use plastic freezer wrap, freezer-coated paper, and plastic freezer bags to rewrap these products in meal-size or single-size portions. Separate chops, steaks, ground meat patties, or chicken parts and wrap individually before freezing. Pack into plastic freezer bags once frozen. Fresh meat and poultry can be frozen for up to three months.

Either freeze fresh ready-made stock from the chilled sections in supermarkets and gourmet shops or make a simple stock of your own (see page 154 for simple chicken stock). Freeze any type of stock in small quantities of about 1 cup per plastic freezer bag. Or freeze in ice-cube trays until solid, then transfer to a plastic freezer bag. One ice cube is the equivalent of about 2 tablespoons in volume, so eight ice cubes will give you 1 cup of stock. To thaw, either place in the fridge for at least 2 hours, or place in a small pot and heat very gently until melted; bring to a boil, reduce the heat, and simmer for 5 minutes before using. Freeze for up to one month.

Bread such as pita bread, sliced bread, rolls, bagels, and loaves all freeze well, but don't just throw them into the freezer in their original packaging, which can cause ice crystals to build up in the bag. Instead, rewrap them in another plastic freezer bag as well. Before you freeze them, slice whole loaves and cut bagels in half so you can toast them straight from the freezer. Bread can be frozen for about six weeks.

Most natural hard **cheeses** freeze well. Cheddar, Edam, Gouda, Swiss, pecorino romano, and Parmesan should be cut into small blocks about 1 inch × 4 inches. Wrap each block with freezer paper and then heavy-duty foil. Thaw in the refrigerator for 4 to 6 hours until ice free (you can grate the pecorino and Parmesan straight from the freezer). The cheese may look a little mottled in color but that's just due to surface moisture. All these cheeses can be stored for up to four months. Blue cheese such as Roquefort and Stilton can be stored for up to three months. It may become a bit more crumbly but it is good for salads. Vacuum-packed sliced cheeses can be stored for up to one month.

Butter and margarine can be frozen in the packaging and then inserted into a plastic freezer bag. They can be stored for up to six months. Thaw in the fridge. Whipped butters and spreads, however, tend to break down, causing the product to separate.

Nuts that have not been toasted deteriorate quickly in the cupboard, even if they are kept in plastic bags or airtight containers, so freeze them instead. Place in plastic freezer bags, then in a freezer-safe plastic container in the freezer. This prevents any chance of odors seeping in and also prevents them from being crushed by other frozen foods. Freeze for up to six weeks. **Praline** (nuts coated in caramelized sugar, then smashed; see page 198) can pep up ice cream sundaes and cakes and add the final touch to a dessert. Freeze for up to six weeks.

Special ingredients that may have required a special trip to Chinatown or Little India can be frozen and used when needed. Whole ginger, galangal, kaffir lime leaves, and lemongrass all freeze well, as do fresh curry leaves and fresh turmeric. Wrap in plastic freezer wrap, then either place in a plastic freezer bag or cover with heavy-duty foil.

Tropical fruits such as papaya, mangoes, and passion fruit can all be processed into a puree, frozen in ice-cube trays until solid, then transferred to plastic freezer bags for use in shakes or fruit cocktails. Fresh grated coconut freezes really well. To crack open easily, preheat the oven to 350°F. Put a hole in the coconut to drain the water (remember that this is not milk) out of the fruit and place the whole thing in the oven for 20 minutes. Allow to cool, then crack open with a hammer—the flesh comes clean away from the shell. Peel the brown skin from the coconut and shred the coconut on a box grater. To freeze, spread on a baking sheet lined with plastic wrap and freeze until solid, about 1 hour. Transfer to a plastic freezer bag. Freeze for up to three weeks. Use directly from the freezer in and on cakes, or toast for rice pilafs. Open freeze (dry freeze) leftover berries until solid, then pack them in bags. Again, use them for shakes and fruit juices or as fruit ice cubes in cocktails. Excess lemon and lime juice can be frozen in ice-cube trays until solid, then stored in plastic freezer bags, perfect to use in teas or mixed drinks. Freeze fruits for up to six weeks.

foods that don't freeze well

Dairy such as milk, cream, buttermilk, sour cream, and yogurt ideally should not be frozen, as they separate and the flavor alters.

Eggs cannot be frozen in their shells but you can crack them into a container and freeze them. If you are making meringues, you can freeze the remaining yolks; however, add 1 teaspoon sugar or ¼ teaspoon salt per yolk (of course, depending on end use). Make sure you freeze the egg yolks in quantities that can be used directly in baking or making custards for tarts. Cooked eggs cannot be frozen.

Mayonnaise should not be frozen, as the emulsion will break down and separate.

Cured meats such as bacon, ham, and smoked or dried sausages are not recommended for freezing, as the saltiness can cause an unpleasant aftertaste. If an unopened vacuum-sealed pack is frozen, it will be okay for up to one month.

Fresh **cabbage**, **celery**, **salad greens**, and **tomatoes** are too watery to freeze well. Upon thawing, the cells break down and turn to mush.

There has been some debate about whether **coffee beans** can be frozen, and the consensus seems to be that they should not be. Any moisture among the coffee beans or, even worse, in ready-ground coffee, will make it go stale very quickly. You can freeze coffee that is vacuum-sealed, but once opened, it is hard to keep out moisture. Once the bag is opened, store the coffee in a well-sealed container in the refrigerator.

Freezing raw ingredients such as meat, chicken, or fish in a marinade is ideal for last-minute meals. These creative, make-ahead dishes, once thawed, can be stir-fried, roasted, broiled, or grilled. While thawing, the meat, chicken, or fish is imbued with the marinade, which imparts flavor and tenderizes as needed.

It is important to start with fresh meat, chicken, or fish that has not already been frozen. Once the meat, chicken, or fish is added to a marinade, freeze the food in small portions, such as two servings in each plastic bag. Remove the bag(s) from the freezer the evening before or the morning of the day you want to serve the food and thaw in the refrigerator. For meatballs or dumplings, there is a whole variety of different cooking methods and recipes to suit you and your family.

raw freeze

stir-fries

Stir-fries cook in no time, but they can be time consuming when it comes to chopping and marinating. If meat is sliced, frozen in its marinade, and thawed, more than half the work is done, and all you have to do on the day of serving is chop two to three vegetables and stir-fry everything together for a few minutes.

I use a wok when stir-frying, because the wok's depth and sloped sides contain the food better while stirring. Use a wok with a flat bottom; it will sit more comfortably on the stove. You can also stir-fry in a large nonstick skillet if you don't have a wok.

SERVES 2 TO 4

FREEZE FOR UP TO 4 WEEKS

preparing chicken, pork, and beef for stir-fries

Once the meat of your choice is prepared, choose one of the recommended marinades. Then once the meat is thawed, add 2 to 3 vegetables listed on page 27 and stir-fry as directed. Each marinade provides enough for ¾ pound of meat or chicken, which serves two. To serve four, double the marinade and meat and pack in two plastic freezer bags for quicker thawing.

Chicken: Use boneless, skinless chicken breasts. Separate the tender fillet under the chicken breast with a paring knife. Working with one piece at a time, place the chicken breast and the tender between sheets of plastic wrap or parchment paper and flatten with a meat mallet or rolling pin until about ¼ inch thick. Remove the paper and thinly slice the meat into ¼-inch-wide, 2-inch-long strips.

Pork: Use tenderloin. Use a paring knife to remove any fat and sinew from the tenderloin. Cut the tenderloin in half lengthwise to create two long pieces. Place the two pieces between sheets of plastic wrap or parchment paper and flatten with a meat mallet or rolling pin until about ¼ inch thick. Remove the paper and slice the meat into ¼-inch-wide, 3-inch-long strips.

Beef: Use steaks such as sirloin, rib-eye, London broil, shell, or skirt. Sirloin or rib-eye are both tender cuts, and a good rib-eye steak will have marbling. Flatten between sheets of plastic wrap or parchment paper with a meat mallet or rolling pin until ¼ inch thick. Slice across the grain into strips ⅛ inch wide and 3 to 4 inches long.

For London broil and shell steaks, trim any visible fat, place the meat between two sheets of plastic wrap or parchment paper, and flatten with a meat mallet until ¼ inch thick. Cutting across the grain, at an angle, slice into thin strips about ¼ inch wide and 4 to 5 inches long.

Skirt steak is rather thin and doesn't require flattening. Just cut across the grain at an angle into ½-inch-wide, 3- to 4-inch-long strips.

marinades for stir-fries

Each recipe provides enough marinade for ³/₄ pound of meat or chicken, which serves two. To serve four, double the marinade and meat.

GINGER-SESAME MARINADE

3 tablespoons rice wine

1 teaspoon sugar

1 teaspoon toasted sesame oil

2 teaspoons chopped fresh ginger

Whisk together all ingredients in a bowl.

OYSTER SAUCE AND GARLIC MARINADE

3 tablespoons rice wine

2 tablespoons oyster sauce

1 tablespoon hoisin sauce

2 teaspoons peanut oil

2 garlic cloves, thinly sliced

Whisk together all ingredients in a bowl.

HOISIN-SHERRY MARINADE

3 tablespoons dry sherry

2 teaspoons honey

2 teaspoons tomato paste

2 tablespoons hoisin sauce

1 tablespoon peanut oil

Whisk together all ingredients in a bowl.

BLACK BEAN AND CHILE MARINADE

2 tablespoons rice wine

1 tablespoon sugar

2-inch piece fresh ginger,
   peeled and cut into thin slices

2 garlic cloves, sliced

2 tablespoons salted black beans, rinsed,
   drained, and coarsely chopped

1 small red chile, finely sliced

1 teaspoon toasted sesame oil

1 tablespoon low-sodium soy sauce

Whisk together all ingredients in a bowl.

To freeze: Once the marinade is prepared, add the chicken or the meat of your choice and coat to mix. Once coated, transfer the entire mixture to one (if serving two) or two (if serving four) 1-quart plastic freezer bag(s) and seal, pressing out as much air as possible. Flatten the bag(s), spreading out the mixture to a single layer, and freeze for 1 hour until solid. Repack in the freezer.

To thaw: If you are in a hurry, thaw the bag(s) of meat or chicken completely immersed in a bowl of ice cold water for 1 to 2 hours, per the instructions on page 12, until the bag feels soft and ice free. Or place the bag on a plate and thaw in the refrigerator for at least 4 hours or overnight. Allow the meat to stand at room temperature for 15 minutes before cooking.

VEGETABLE PREPARATION

Choose two or more of the following vegetables for the stir-fry:

1 large carrot, peeled and cut into matchsticks

1 pound bok choy or Chinese mustard leaves,
   trimmed and cut into 1-inch pieces if large;
   baby bok choy can be left whole

1 pound broccoli rabe, trimmed and cut into 1- to
   3-inch lengths

6 ounces fresh baby corn

8 ounces fresh shiitake mushrooms, stems
   discarded, wiped clean, and left whole or thinly
   sliced

1 bunch scallions, white parts only, cut into 2- to
   3-inch lengths

8 ounces sugar snap peas

8 ounces snow peas

8 ounces green beans, trimmed and cut into
   2-inch lengths

Basic Stir-Fry

1 bag marinated meat or chicken,
  thawed (see page 27)

3 tablespoons peanut oil

2 to 3 vegetables (from the list
  on page 27)

1 to 2 tablespoons soy sauce

Rice or noodles for serving

SERVES 2

1. Transfer the contents of the bag to a bowl and use a slotted spoon to transfer the meat or chicken to a plate. Reserve the marinade.

2. Heat a wok or large skillet over medium-high heat until hot. Add 2 tablespoons of the oil. Add the vegetables to the wok, first the tougher ones, such as carrots, broccoli, rabe, and mushrooms, as they need more cooking time, then the snow peas, sugar snaps, and scallions toward the end of cooking. Stir-fry by lifting and tossing the vegetables for 3 to 5 minutes until tender but still crisp. With a slotted spoon, transfer to a bowl and set aside.

3. Wipe the wok or skillet clean with a paper towel and heat the remaining oil until smoking. Add the meat or chicken and stir-fry for 3 to 4 minutes until seared all over and browned.

4. Return the vegetables to the wok, along with the reserved marinade and soy sauce. Stir-fry for another 2 minutes or until the juices are bubbling. The juices must come to a boil and bubble for at least 2 minutes. Serve immediately with rice or noodles.

roasting, broiling, and grilling

Meat, chicken, and fish can be frozen in a marinade or dry rub. Upon thawing, the marinade or rub will tenderize and flavor the meat, which can then be grilled, broiled, or roasted.

SERVES 4

FREEZE FOR UP TO 5 WEEKS

preparing fish, chicken, pork, lamb, and beef

To serve four, allow four 7-ounce chicken breasts, lamb chops, pork chops, or beef or fish steaks, or 1½ pounds prepared kebab chunks for each of the following marinades. If you are preparing kebabs, you will need about 2 pounds of meat, poultry, or fish for four servings, enough to thread onto eight skewers. Do not freeze with skewers.

Fish Steaks or Fillets: Choose firm fish, such as salmon, cod, halibut, swordfish, monkfish, and tuna that has not been frozen previously. Choose only the thicker part of the fillet for steaks or fillets. To make boneless fish steaks, cut the thicker part of a fillet from salmon or cod and cut into ½-inch-thick slices; fold the fish into a horseshoe with the skin now inside the horseshoe and secure with a toothpick—this is excellent for broiling and grilling. For kebabs, choose tuna, salmon, monkfish, cod, or halibut, remove the skin and bones, and be sure to cut into at least 1- to 1½-inch-thick chunks. Fish steaks and fillets can be frozen in a marinade or rub for up to 3 weeks.

Chicken: If you are planning to grill or broil chicken, use skinless, boneless breasts. With a paring knife, remove the tender on the underside of the breast (use the tender for kebabs). Place the chicken breast between sheets of plastic wrap or parchment and flatten with a meat mallet or rolling pin until about ½ inch thick. For roasting, you can also use skin-on, bone-in breasts, legs, and thighs. For kebabs, use tenders or skinless, boneless thigh or breast meat cut into 1-inch chunks. Chicken can be frozen in a marinade or rub for up to 5 weeks.

Pork: Use center cut pork loin chops, center cut boneless loin chops, tenderloin, back ribs, country-style ribs, spareribs, or cubed steak from the leg. For kebabs, use trimmed pork tenderloin and cubed steak cut into 1-inch chunks. Pork can be frozen in a marinade or rub for up to 3 weeks.

Lamb: Choose chops from the loin, rib, and shoulder. For kebabs, opt for cubed leg of lamb and lamb tenderloin cut into 1½-inch chunks. Lamb can be frozen in a marinade or rub for up to 3 weeks.

Beef: For grilling, choose rib-eye, New York strip, porterhouse, T-bone, tenderloin tails, or tips. Top round/London broil, skirt, flank, and hanger steak must be tenderized with a marinade or rub. For kebabs, cut up rib-eye or shell steaks into 1½-inch chunks. Beef can be frozen in a marinade or rub for up to 3 weeks.

marinades and rubs for pan-searing, roasting, broiling, and grilling

EACH MARINADE SERVES 4

Mediterranean Marinade

1 teaspoon grated lemon zest

¼ cup lemon juice

¼ cup olive oil

1 garlic clove, sliced

3 rosemary or thyme sprigs

½ teaspoon black peppercorns, roughly crushed

Whisk together all ingredients in a bowl.

Moroccan Marinade

1 large preserved lemon (see Glossary), soaked in
   warm water for 30 minutes

1 tablespoon coriander seeds

2 teaspoons cumin seeds

1 teaspoon sugar

1 teaspoon sea salt

1 teaspoon smoked paprika (see page 205)

2 garlic cloves, finely chopped

1 tablespoon olive oil

Drain the lemon and wash under cold water to remove the salty taste. Halve the lemon and discard any seeds, finely dice, and place in a bowl. Heat a heavy skillet until hot, then add the coriander and cumin seeds and cook until lightly toasted, swirling the pan to keep the seeds turning, about 2 minutes. Cool slightly, then put in a spice blender with the sugar and salt and blend until finely ground. Add the spice mix to the lemon with the paprika, garlic, and oil; mix well.

> *continued*

Chipotle Adobo and Lime Rub

2 tablespoons adobo sauce from canned
   chipotles in adobo sauce
Juice from 2 limes
1 tablespoon light oil such as safflower oil
$\frac{1}{2}$ teaspoon kosher salt

Whisk together all ingredients in a bowl.

Jerk Seasoning Rub

1 teaspoon allspice berries
1 cinnamon stick
$\frac{1}{2}$ teaspoon black peppercorns
1 tablespoon dark brown sugar
1 teaspoon sea salt flakes
$\frac{1}{8}$ teaspoon cayenne pepper
1 tablespoon peanut oil
2 tablespoons lime juice

Put the allspice, cinnamon, and peppercorns in a spice grinder and grind. In a bowl mix the ground spices with the sugar, salt, cayenne, oil, and lime juice.

To freeze: Once the marinade or rub is prepared, add the meat, chicken, or fish of your choice to the marinade or rub and coat to mix. Once coated, transfer the entire mixture to two 1-quart plastic freezer bags and seal, pressing out as much air as possible. Flatten the bags, spreading out the mixture in a single layer, and freeze until solid, about $1\frac{1}{2}$ hours. Repack in the freezer.

To Thaw: Place the bags of marinated or rubbed meat, chicken, or fish on a plate and thaw in the refrigerator for 4 hours or overnight. Let stand at room temperature for 15 minutes before cooking. Or if you are short on time, thaw the bags completely immersed in a bowl of ice-cold water for 2 hours.

For kebabs, soak bamboo skewers for at least 20 minutes before using so they don't burn. Take care not to thread the chunks too closely together on the skewers, as they need the space to cook evenly.

roasting

Preheat the oven to 400°F. Place a rack in the top of the oven. You will not need to turn over the steaks or chicken breasts during cooking, although you could baste with any marinade or rub remaining in the bag.

Fish Steaks or Fillets: Salmon and white fish steaks will require about 20 minutes. Fillets will take 15 to 20 minutes, depending on the thickness.

Chicken: Single chicken breasts on the bone will need 30 to 35 minutes; single chicken breasts off the bone, weighing around 7 ounces, will require 20 to 25 minutes.

Pork: For baby back ribs, allow about 45 minutes, turning once and basting with any remaining marinade. For large, country-style ribs, cover for the first 30 minutes of cooking, then cook uncovered for another 30 minutes.

Lamb: For top-end shoulder chops, allow about 10 minutes for medium rare, 15 minutes for well done. Lamb rib and loin chops will require about 30 minutes.

broiling

Preheat the broiler for at least 5 minutes. Place a rack on the broiling pan and place under the broiler to preheat. The chops and steaks will stick to the rack unless the rack is preheated. There is no need to oil the rack. Baste the fish, chicken, or meat with any leftover marinade or rub.

Fish Steaks or Fillets: Cook for 5 to 8 minutes on each side.

Chicken Breasts: Cook for 8 minutes on each side.

Pork Chops: Cook for 10 minutes on each side.

Lamb: For thick chops, cook for 8 minutes on each side for medium rare and 10 minutes for well done. Lamb chops from the top end of the shoulder will require 3 minutes on each side.

Steaks: Cook 4 minutes on each side for rare, 5 minutes on each side for medium rare, or 8 minutes on each side for well done.

grilling

Once the charcoal is lit and the flames have subsided, spread the coals in the barbecue. Place the grill rack about 6 inches above the charcoal. Let preheat for at least 10 minutes. Carefully oil the grill by using tongs to wipe down the grill rack with oiled paper towels. Alternatively, halve a large potato, hold with tongs, dip the cut side in oil, then rub over the grill. This will prevent the meat, chicken, or fish from sticking. Once the coals are white hot and the flames have completely subsided, place the prepared food on the grill rack. Baste with leftover marinade while cooking.

Fish Steaks or Fillets: Cook for 3 to 5 minutes on each side. The salmon steaks should still be slightly pink in the center. The tuna steaks should cook for only 2 minutes on each side, as they are perfect when rare. If you prefer tuna to be well done, then go with 4 minutes on each side. Allow about 10 minutes total cooking time for white fish or salmon kebabs.

Chicken: Cook for 5 minutes on each side for boneless chicken breasts. For kebabs using thigh meat, allow 30 minutes total cooking time; allow 20 minutes for breast meat, turning several times.

Pork: Center cut pork chops will require at least 10 minutes on each side, until just slightly pink in the center. Allow 15 to 18 minutes total cooking time for kebabs, turning several times. For ribs, allow 40 minutes total cooking time, turning several times, and sometimes pulling them out to the side before putting back over the hottest part of the barbecue.

Lamb: For a ¾- to 1-inch thickness, allow about 3 minutes on each side until seared and browned on the outside yet still rare in the center. For well done cook for 5 to 6 minutes on each side. For lamb chops from the top end of the shoulder, allow about 2 minutes on each side. For small lamb ribs, allow about 25 minutes. For kebabs, allow 10 to 15 minutes total cooking time, turning several times.

Steaks: For a ¾- to 1-inch thickness, allow about 3 minutes on each side until seared and browned on the outside yet still rare in the center. For well done cook for 5 to 6 minutes on each side. For kebabs, allow 8 to 10 minutes total cooking time, turning several times.

using a grill pan

Come rain or shine, you can still grill any of these marinated cuts using a grill pan.

To help prevent sticking, heat a griddle or grill pan over high heat until very hot. Use a paper towel to rub with oil and salt; heat for 1 minute. Remove the salt. Once the pan is smoking—and it must be really hot—add your chosen marinated cut. Baste with leftover marinade while cooking.

Fish Steaks or Fillets: Cook for 4 to 5 minutes on each side, remembering that the fish should still be juicy inside. Tuna should not be cooked for more than 2 minutes on each side for medium rare.

Chicken Breast: Cook for 4 minutes on each side for prepared boneless breasts, about 15 minutes for chicken breast kebabs, or 20 minutes for dark meat.

Pork Chops: Cook for 12 minutes on each side, turning at least four times. Allow 15 minutes for kebabs.

Beef or Lamb: Cook for at least 2 minutes on each side for rare, 3 minutes on each side for medium, or 5 minutes on each side for well done. Allow the same cooking times for lamb and beef kebabs.

Cutlets in Marsala Sauce

The cutlets need to be very thin, about ¼ inch thick; this allows them to be cooked from frozen. The prepared cutlets can be thawed and then cooked if you prefer.

CHICKEN OR PORK

½ teaspoon crushed red pepper

Finely grated zest of 1 lemon

2 tablespoons extra virgin olive oil

8 chicken or pork cutlets

8 thin slices prosciutto di Parma

2 tablespoons all-purpose flour

Salt and freshly ground black
   pepper

1 cup sweet Marsala

1 tablespoon capers

2 tablespoons butter

¼ cup chopped fresh flat-leaf
   parsley

SERVES 4

FREEZE FOR UP TO 4 WEEKS

1. Mix the red pepper, lemon zest, and 1 tablespoon of the oil in a small bowl and rub it all over the cutlets. Wrap each cutlet with a slice of prosciutto.

2. Place the flour on a flat plate and season with salt and pepper. Coat each cutlet with flour, dusting off the excess.

3. Heat the remaining oil in a large skillet, add the cutlets (in two batches if necessary), and cook for 3 minutes on each side or until soft all the way through and seared on the outside. Remove and keep warm while cooking the second batch.

4. Add the Marsala to the pan juice and let bubble for 2 minutes; add the capers and cook for 1 minute. Stir in the butter, then return the chicken or pork to the pan, turning in the sauce. Cook for 2 minutes, then sprinkle the parsley on top and serve.

> *continued*

LAMB

1 teaspoon dried herbes de
    Provence or mixture of
    rosemary, oregano, and
    marjoram

1 teaspoon crushed red pepper

¼ cup extra virgin olive oil

8 lamb cutlets

2 tablespoons all-purpose flour

1 cup sweet Marsala

2 tablespoons butter

3 tablespoons chopped fresh
    oregano

1. Mix the herbes de Provence with the red pepper and 1 tablespoon of the olive oil. Rub all over the lamb.

2. Dust the lamb with the flour. Heat the remaining oil in the skillet until hot and sear the lamb for 1 minute on each side (in two batches if necessary) or until soft all the way through and seared on the outside. Remove the cutlets and set aside.

3. Add the Marsala to the pan juices and let bubble for 2 to 3 minutes until reduced by half. Stir in the butter. Return the cutlets to the pan and turn to coat with the sauce. Add the oregano and cook for 1 minute. The lamb should still be slightly pink. Serve.

To freeze: Wrap each prepared, uncooked cutlet in plastic freezer wrap and place on a baking sheet. Freeze until solid, about 1 hour. Pack the frozen cutlets in a plastic freezer bag and return to the freezer.

To cook: Cook straight from the freezer. Unwrap each cutlet and coat with flour. Cook the chicken or pork for 5 minutes on each side and continue as in the recipe on page 37. For the lamb, cook for 2 minutes on each side, then continue as in the above recipe.

burgers

Serve these chicken, turkey, beef, and lamb burgers on traditional sesame rolls with grilled red onions, sliced tomatoes, shredded lettuce, spicy ketchup, and pickles. The lamb burgers can be served in toasted pita breads with chopped cucumber and tomato salad, olives, and pickled sweet green chiles.

EACH RECIPE MAKES 4 BURGERS

FREEZE FOR UP TO 2 MONTHS

CHICKEN OR TURKEY BURGERS

One ½-inch-thick slice rustic white bread with
    crusts removed, torn into pieces

⅓ cup milk

¾ pound boneless, skinless chicken breast, cut
    into small pieces

¾ pound boneless, skinless chicken thighs, cut
    into small pieces, or 1¼ pounds ground turkey
    meat and ¼ pound chopped bacon

1 small onion, finely chopped

2 tablespoons fresh thyme leaves, finely chopped

Grated zest of 1 lemon

Salt and freshly ground black pepper

2 teaspoons olive oil

BEEF BURGERS

One ½-inch-thick slice rustic white bread with
    crusts removed, torn into pieces

⅓ cup milk

1½ pounds ground beef chuck

1 small onion, finely chopped

2 tablespoons chopped fresh flat-leaf parsley

3 tablespoons Worcestershire sauce

Salt and freshly ground black pepper

1 to 2 teaspoons olive oil

LAMB AND FETA BURGERS

One ½-inch-thick slice rustic white bread with
    crusts removed, torn into pieces

⅓ cup milk

1 pound ground lamb

¼ pound ground pork

1 small onion, finely chopped

2 teaspoons dried mint

2 tablespoons chopped fresh flat-leaf parsley

Freshly ground black pepper

1 teaspoon olive oil

3 ounces Greek feta, crumbled

1. Soak the bread in milk for 10 minutes. If using chicken, place in a food processor and process for 2 minutes until ground.

2. Put the meat in a bowl and add the onion, herbs, and seasonings. Drain the bread, squeezing out the milk. Add the bread to the meat mixture. Add the oil and mix gently but do not squeeze the mixture between your fingers. You need to keep the mixture light, with pockets of air to ensure the burgers do not become too dense and dry when cooked.

> *continued*

3. Form the chicken, turkey, or beef into 4 large patties, about 4 inches wide by $^{3}/_{4}$ to 1 inch thick. If not planning to freeze, place on a baking sheet lined with plastic wrap and refrigerate for 30 minutes, then cook. For the lamb burgers, divide the mixture into 4 parts. Shape each into a ball. Make a hole deep into the center and fill with feta cheese. Close the space and press down gently to form a patty about 3½ inches wide and about $^{3}/_{4}$ inch thick. If not planning to freeze, place on a baking sheet lined with plastic wrap and refrigerate for 30 minutes, then cook.

To freeze: Line a baking sheet with plastic wrap and place the burgers on it, allowing about 1 inch between them. Open freeze until solid, about 1½ hours. Once solid, stack the burgers with squares of freezer paper or plastic wrap between each patty, so that you will be able to separate the frozen burgers. Wrap tightly with plastic freezer wrap. Alternatively, wrap each frozen burger tightly with plastic freezer wrap and place in a plastic freezer bag. (The frozen burgers can also be heat sealed once solid). Return to the freezer.

To cook from frozen: Preheat the oven to 400°F. Preheat a grill pan or skillet. Brush the grill pan with oil or add about 1 teaspoon oil to the skillet. Add the beef burgers and cook for 2 minutes on each side. Finish off in the oven for another 10 minutes for medium rare. For chicken or turkey burgers, cook for 8 minutes on each side, then for 10 minutes in the oven. For lamb burgers, cook for 5 minutes on each side, then for 5 minutes in the oven.

To cook after thawing: Remove the wrapping from the frozen burgers and place on a baking sheet lined with paper towels. Thaw in the fridge for 2 hours. Preheat a grill pan or skillet; brush the grill pan with oil or add about 1 teaspoon oil to the skillet. For beef burgers, cook for 5 minutes on each side for medium rare; 4 minutes on each side for lamb burgers; 8 minutes on each side for chicken or turkey burgers. To barbecue, allow 6 to 8 minutes on each side for beef burgers for medium rare; 8 to 10 minutes on each side for lamb burgers; and 18 minutes on each side for chicken burgers.

meatballs

Meatballs are loved by all. Each family has a traditional recipe and many evoke fond childhood memories. For a light airy texture, gently mix the meatball mixture with your hands, and try to avoid squeezing the mixture between your fingers. To prevent the meatballs from sticking to your palms while shaping, keep your hands just slightly wet.

Freeze the meatballs raw, then use straight from the freezer or thawed in the recipes that follow.

EACH RECIPE MAKES 20 MEATBALLS

FREEZE FOR UP TO 1 MONTH

Chicken Meatballs

Chicken meatballs can be used whenever beef meatballs are called for. They can also be used with Asian ingredients for a stir-fry or noodle soup.

One 1½-inch-thick slice rustic bread with crust removed, torn into very small pieces

⅓ cup milk

1 pound boneless, skinless chicken breast

2 ounces (4 tablespoons) pancetta or bacon, finely chopped

1 small onion, finely chopped

1 tablespoon chopped fresh flat-leaf parsley

1 teaspoon fennel seeds, roughly crushed with a mortar and pestle

1 teaspoon crushed red pepper, optional

1 large egg, lightly beaten

1 tablespoon olive oil

1. Place the bread and milk in a bowl and let sit for 10 minutes or until all the milk is soaked up.

2. Place the chicken and pancetta in a food processor and pulse until the meat is ground. Transfer to a large mixing bowl. Add the onion, parsley, fennel seeds, and red pepper, if using. Mix gently with your hands, being careful not to squeeze the mixture. Add the egg and oil and continue to mix. Finally, add the bread mixture and combine.

3. Form twenty 1½-inch balls from the mixture. Cook or freeze, using the directions on page 46.

Lamb Meatballs

Adding a little pork to the lamb mixture produces a light and juicy texture.

One 1½-inch-thick slice rustic
    bread with crust removed, torn
    into very small pieces

⅓ cup milk

¾ pound ground lamb

¼ pound ground pork

1 small onion, finely chopped

1 garlic clove, lightly smashed

Salt and freshly ground black
    pepper

1 teaspoon dried oregano

1 large egg, lightly beaten

1 tablespoon olive oil

1. Place the bread and milk in a bowl and let sit for 10 minutes or until all the milk is soaked up.

2. Place the ground lamb, ground pork, onion, garlic, salt and pepper to taste, and oregano in a large bowl and mix gently with your hands, being careful not to squeeze the mixture. Add the egg and oil and continue to mix. Finally, add the bread mixture and combine.

3. Form twenty 1½-inch balls from the mixture. Cook or freeze, using the directions on page 46.

Beef Meatballs

These are traditional Italian-style meatballs, perfect cooked in a tomato sauce and served with pasta. They can also be used in pasta bakes.

One 1½-inch-thick slice rustic bread with crust removed, torn into very small pieces

⅓ cup milk

1 pound ground beef chuck

1 small onion, finely chopped

2 tablespoons chopped fresh flat-leaf parsley

3 tablespoons finely grated fresh Parmesan

Salt and freshly ground black pepper

1 large egg, lightly beaten

1 tablespoon olive oil

1. Place the bread and the milk in a bowl and let sit for 10 minutes or until all the milk is soaked up.

2. Place the ground beef, onion, parsley, Parmesan, and salt and pepper to taste in a bowl. Mix well with your hands, but do not squeeze the mixture. Add the egg and oil and continue to mix. Finally, add the bread mixture and combine.

3. Form twenty 1½-inch balls from the mixture.

To freeze: Line a large baking sheet with plastic wrap and arrange the meatballs, keeping them spaced well apart, about 1 inch. Open freeze until solid, about 1½ hours. Place the meatballs in a plastic freezer bag or a freezer-safe container. Alternatively, heat seal in batches of six. Return to the freezer.

To thaw: Some of the recipes require the meatballs to be thawed; for others, you can cook the meatballs directly from the freezer. For those that require thawing, line a baking sheet with paper towels and place the required amount of meatballs on top. Cover loosely with plastic wrap. Place in the refrigerator for 3 hours or overnight.

Chinese Meatball and Noodle Soup

2 tablespoons red or white miso paste

1 tablespoon soy sauce

2 tablespoons mirin

20 chicken meatballs, frozen

1 bunch scallions, light green and white parts only, cut into 2-inch lengths and then cut in half lengthwise

2 large carrots, peeled and cut into thin 2-inch lengths

1/2 head Napa cabbage, finely shredded

1/2 pound ramen noodles, fresh or dried

Chile garlic sauce (sambal oelek), soy sauce, and toasted sesame oil for serving

SERVES 4

1. Bring a large pot of salted water to a boil.

2. Place the miso, 1 quart water, the soy sauce, and mirin in a separate pot and bring to a boil. Drop the meatballs in and return to a boil. Reduce the heat to a simmer and cook the meatballs for 10 minutes or until almost cooked through.

3. Add the scallions and carrots to the soup and cook for another 5 minutes or until the meatballs are cooked through. Add the cabbage.

4. Quickly add the noodles to the pot of boiling water, stirring to separate the noodles. Cook for 3 minutes or as directed on the package. Drain and divide the noodles among four large deep serving bowls. Ladle the meatballs, vegetables, and broth on top. Serve with chile garlic sauce, soy sauce, and toasted sesame oil.

Get Better Chicken Noodle Soup

Every grandmother has her version of comforting chicken noodle soup. Both my grandmothers always boiled a chicken and used the stock to cook the macaroni. The chicken was then shredded and returned to the pasta and stock and served with finely grated halloumi cheese. This version is the Jewish-American and Italian-American version rolled into one!

1 quart chicken stock

2 large carrots, peeled and diced

1 large onion, halved and cut into
 ½-inch wedges

20 chicken meatballs, frozen

2 ounces vermicelli noodles

Salt and freshly ground black
 pepper

2 tablespoons chopped fresh flat-
 leaf parsley, optional

SERVES 4

1. Place the chicken stock, carrots, and onion in a large pot and bring to a boil. Gently ease the meatballs into the pot and return to a boil. Reduce the heat and cook for 15 minutes or until the meatballs are cooked through. Remove the meatballs from the broth and set aside.

2. Add the vermicelli and salt and pepper to taste to the stock and vegetables; return to a boil and stir. Cook for 5 minutes or until the vegetables are tender. Return the meatballs to the pot with the parsley (if using) and stir. Cook for another 2 minutes to heat the meatballs through. Taste and adjust the seasoning. Serve in small bowls.

Meatballs in Tomato Sauce

¼ cup olive oil

20 beef, chicken, or lamb
meatballs, thawed if frozen

2 cups Basic Tomato Sauce,
thawed if frozen (page 69)

Salt and freshly ground black
pepper

1 pound spaghetti

Freshly grated Parmesan for
serving

SERVES 4

1. Heat the oil over medium heat in a skillet large enough
to hold the meatballs in a single layer. Add the meatballs
and cook for 10 minutes or until brown all over. Add
the sauce, increase the heat, and bring to a boil. Reduce
the heat, cover, and simmer for 25 minutes or until the
oil separates from the tomatoes and the sauce is slightly
thickened. Taste and season with salt and pepper.

2. Meanwhile, bring a large pot of salted water to a boil.
Add the spaghetti and return to a boil. Cook for
12 minutes or until the pasta is al dente. Drain,
reserving about ½ cup of the pasta cooking water.
Transfer the meatballs from the sauce to a serving
platter. Add the pasta to the tomato sauce and toss to
coat, adding a little of the pasta water to thin the sauce
if needed. Serve the pasta with the meatballs on the
side. Serve with Parmesan and black pepper.

Meatball Pasta Bake

12 ounces pasta shells

5 tablespoons olive oil

20 beef, chicken, or lamb
meatballs, thawed if frozen

2 cups Basic Tomato Sauce,
thawed (page 69)

6 ounces fresh mozzarella, thinly
sliced

3 tablespoons finely grated fresh
Parmesan

Freshly ground black pepper

SERVES 4

1. Preheat the oven to 375°F. Place a rack in the center of the oven.

2. Bring a large pot of salted water to a boil. Add the pasta and return to a boil. Cook for about 10 minutes; the pasta should be underdone. Drain the pasta, reserving 1 cup of the pasta cooking water.

3. Heat ¼ cup of the oil over medium heat in a skillet large enough to hold the meatballs in a single layer. Add the meatballs and cook for 10 minutes or until brown all over. Add the tomato sauce, increase the heat, and bring to a boil. Reduce the heat and simmer, covered, for 10 minutes.

4. Place the drained pasta in a large ovenproof baking dish, no more than 2 inches deep, and drizzle with the remaining oil. Carefully spoon in the meatballs and sauce and mix slightly with the pasta, adding some of the reserved pasta water to thin the sauce if necessary. Cover with the sliced mozzarella. Sprinkle with the Parmesan and black pepper.

5. Bake for 30 minutes or until the cheese is bubbling and golden brown. Allow the bake to stand for 10 minutes before serving.

Chicken Meatball Stir-Fry

5 tablespoons peanut oil

³/₄ pound fresh shiitake
   mushrooms, stems discarded,
   wiped clean, and sliced

½ pound bok choy, thinly sliced

20 chicken meatballs, thawed if
   frozen

1 tablespoon hoisin sauce mixed
   with 3 tablespoons water

3 tablespoons soy sauce

1 teaspoon sugar

2 teaspoons cornstarch

2 teaspoons toasted sesame oil

Salt and freshly ground
   black pepper

SERVES 4

1. Heat 2 tablespoons of the peanut oil in a wok or skillet over medium-high heat. Stir-fry the mushrooms and bok choy for 3 minutes. Transfer to a plate and set aside.

2. Heat the remaining peanut oil over medium heat. Add the meatballs and brown for 10 minutes, turning frequently. If using a wok, cook the meatballs in batches of six to eight. Add the hoisin sauce mixture to the pan with all the meatballs. Cover and cook over medium heat for 10 minutes.

3. Mix the soy sauce, sugar, and cornstarch in a small bowl until smooth. Return the vegetables to the wok with the cornstarch mixture. Stir-fry for 5 minutes, allowing the sauce to thicken and the meatballs to cook through. Add the toasted sesame oil. Taste and season with salt and pepper.

gyoza

Gyoza, or Japanese dumplings, are pot-stickers filled with chicken, shrimp, or vegetables. Make them ahead, then freeze, and steam, boil, or pan-fry as many as you want directly from the freezer. Serve with one of the dipping sauces on page 59 or poach in miso paste diluted with water. Add some carrots, fresh ginger, or snow peas for flavor.

EACH RECIPE MAKES 44 GYOZA

FREEZE FOR UP TO 4 WEEKS

Shrimp and Pork Gyoza

For shrimp-only gyoza, replace the pork with 4 ounces canned whole water chestnuts, drained and finely chopped, and 2 ounces spinach, cooked, drained, and chopped.

3/4 pound shrimp, peeled, deveined, and coarsely chopped

1/2 pound ground pork

4 scallions, white part only, finely chopped

1 teaspoon grated fresh ginger

2 teaspoons grated lime zest

1 tablespoon cornstarch

2 tablespoons low-sodium soy sauce

1 teaspoon toasted sesame oil

Salt and ground white pepper

One 12-ounce package dumpling wrappers

1. Place the shrimp, ground pork, scallions, ginger, and lime zest in a large bowl. Mix with your hands; do not squeeze the mixture between your fingers. Mix the cornstarch with the soy sauce in a small bowl until smooth. Add to the shrimp mixture. Add the toasted sesame oil. Season with salt and pepper. Mix until combined.

2. Set the wrappers on a clean surface and cover with a damp paper towel while not using. Place one dumpling wrapper on a clean surface and place 1 teaspoon of the shrimp mixture in the center. Moisten the edge of half the circle with water, then bring the ends together to form a semicircle. Starting at one end, twist and fold the edges to secure into a neat crescent; alternatively, pleat the edge to seal. Repeat with the remaining wrappers and filling. Cook or freeze, using the instructions on pages 58–59.

Chicken Gyoza

3/4 pound skinless, boneless
  chicken breast, cut into chunks

6 ounces boneless, skinless chicken
  thighs, cut into chunks

One 8-ounce can whole water
  chestnuts, drained

4 scallions, light green and white
  parts only, coarsely chopped

1 cup fresh cilantro leaves, coarsely
  chopped

1 tablespoon oyster sauce

1 teaspoon brown sugar

1 tablespoon cornstarch

3 tablespoons tamari sauce or low-
  sodium soy sauce

1 teaspoon toasted sesame oil

Salt and ground white pepper

One 12-ounce package dumpling
  wrappers

1. Place the chicken breasts and thighs in a food processor. Pulse to mince. Do not allow a paste to form. Add the water chestnuts and scallions. Pulse once more to finely chop the vegetables.

2. Transfer the chicken mixture to a bowl. Using a fork, stir in the cilantro, oyster sauce, and sugar. Mix the cornstarch with the tamari in a small bowl until smooth, then stir into the chicken mixture. Add the toasted sesame oil and salt and pepper.

3. Set the wrappers on a clean surface and cover with a damp paper towel while not using. Place one dumpling wrapper on a clean surface and place 1 teaspoon of the chicken mixture in the center. Moisten the edge of half the circle with water, then bring the ends together to form a semicircle. Starting at one end, twist and fold the edges to secure into a neat crescent, or pleat the edge to seal. Repeat with the remaining wrappers and filling. Cook or freeze, using the instructions on pages 58–59.

Sesame Vegetable Gyoza

1 large carrot, peeled and coarsely chopped

6 scallions, light green and white parts only, coarsely chopped

One 2-inch piece fresh ginger, peeled and coarsely chopped

One 8-ounce can whole water chestnuts, drained and coarsely chopped

8 ounces spinach, cooked in boiling water and squeezed to remove excess liquid, roughly chopped

1 cup fresh cilantro leaves, roughly chopped

1 tablespoon oyster sauce

1 teaspoon toasted sesame seeds

1 tablespoon cornstarch

2 tablespoons tamari sauce or low-sodium soy sauce

1 teaspoon brown sugar

Salt and ground white pepper

One 12-ounce package dumpling wrappers

1. Place the carrot, scallions, ginger, and water chestnuts in a food processor. Process until the mixture is finely chopped. Add the spinach and pulse two to three more times to combine. Turn out the mixture onto a kitchen towel and squeeze out as much liquid as possible. Place in a mixing bowl. Stir in the cilantro, oyster sauce, and sesame seeds. Mix the cornstarch with the tamari sauce in a small bowl until well blended. Add to the vegetable mixture, along with the sugar and salt and pepper to taste. Stir to combine.

2. Set the wrappers on a clean surface and cover with a damp paper towel while not using. Place one dumpling wrapper on a clean surface and place 1 teaspoon of the vegetable mixture in the center. Moisten half the circle with water, then bring the ends together to form a semicircle. Starting at one end, twist and fold the edges to secure into a neat crescent, or pleat the edges to seal. Repeat with the remaining wrappers and filling. Cook or freeze.

To freeze: Line a baking sheet with plastic wrap and arrange the gyoza in rows, leaving about 1 inch between the dumplings. Freeze until solid, about 2 hours. Transfer to a plastic freezer bag or freezer-safe plastic container; squeeze out as much air as possible when sealing. Alternatively, you can heat seal in batches of eight. Return to the freezer.

LIME AND GINGER

DIPPING SAUCE

Grated zest and juice of 1 lime

1 tablespoon finely chopped fresh
    ginger

1 teaspoon brown sugar

2 tablespoons tamari sauce

1 teaspoon toasted sesame oil

MAKES $1/4$ CUP

Whisk together all ingredients
in a bowl.

HOISIN AND CHILI OIL

1 tablespoon hoisin sauce

3 tablespoons soy sauce

2 tablespoons black vinegar

1 teaspoon chili oil

2 scallions, light green and white
    parts only, finely chopped

2 teaspoons brown sugar

MAKES $1/2$ CUP

Whisk together all ingredients in a
bowl.

To steam: Place a steamer over a pan of simmering water. Lightly brush the steamer with a little vegetable oil. Place at least 8 frozen gyoza in the steamer, keeping them spaced well apart (about $1/2$ inch). Cover and steam for 6 to 8 minutes until tender. Serve with a dipping sauce of your choice.

To pan-fry: Heat a large skillet until hot. Add 1 tablespoon vegetable oil and heat until almost smoking. Add 8 frozen gyoza and cook over low heat for 4 minutes on each side until browned. Raise the heat to medium, add 3 tablespoons water, cover, and cook for an additional 8 to 10 minutes until cooked through; do not be tempted to lift the cover. Serve with a dipping sauce of your choice.

To boil: Bring a large pot of salted water to a boil. Add the dumplings in batches of eight. Cook for 8 minutes or until heated through and the wrapper no longer looks opaque. Drain and serve with a dipping sauce of your choice.

cook once,

This chapter gives leftovers a whole new meaning. The food served on the day of making is transformed for another inspired meal days or weeks later. Sauces for pastas, soups, and bakes are already prepared to make life easier. No need to spend the whole day in the kitchen to create the next five days' worth of meals—simply cook a little extra. Add an extra chicken to the roasting tray and use it to make a Moroccan chicken salad. Poach an extra salmon fillet for fish cakes to be served for next week's lunch. It takes the same amount of time to make one batch of Bolognese or tomato sauce as it does to make two; use extra Bolognese to make a pie, or in the case of the tomato sauce, serve it as a soup, or turn it into four different sauces for pasta. With a little bit of extra effort on the day of cooking, you'll be rewarded with time gained and satisfying results later on.

eat twice

Lemon Roasted Chicken

It takes no more effort to cook two chickens than to cook one. Roast one for dinner and the second for modern Moroccan-style chicken salad for lunch or dinner another day.

4 garlic cloves

Sea salt flakes and freshly ground
　　black pepper

Juice of 1 lemon, squeezed halves
　　reserved

4 tablespoons (½ stick) unsalted
　　butter, softened

Two 3-pound organic chickens, any
　　solid fat around the neck and
　　back cavities removed, washed
　　and patted dry with paper
　　towels

4 large rosemary sprigs

MAKES 2 ROAST CHICKENS

1. Preheat the oven to 375°F. Place a rack in the center of the oven. Place a large roasting rack or wire rack in a large roasting pan.

2. Crush 2 garlic cloves, then mash to a paste with some salt flakes: use a thin-bladed knife to slide along the garlic and salt on the chopping board. Mix the garlic paste, lemon juice, and butter in a small bowl. Season with salt and pepper to taste. Using your hands, gently ease some of the lemon butter between the skin and breast meat of the chickens and rub the rest all over the chickens. Lightly smash the remaining garlic cloves and divide between the main cavities of the chickens. Add the squeezed-out lemon halves and the rosemary to the cavities. Tuck the wing tips under the chicken and tie the legs together.

3. Place the chickens, breast side down, in the roasting pan, and roast for 30 minutes. Turn the chickens over and roast for another 50 minutes. To check for doneness, insert an instant-read thermometer between the thigh and breast. It should register 170°F. Allow to stand for 10 minutes before serving.

Moroccan Chicken Salad

1 large preserved lemon
(see Glossary)

10 saffron strands

½ cup extra virgin olive oil

2 hot red chiles, sliced

1 Lemon Roasted Chicken (page
63) or 2 pounds cooked chicken
meat, skin and bones discarded,
sliced into bite-size pieces

1 pound green beans, trimmed and
blanched for 2 minutes

Chopped fresh cilantro leaves and
flatbread for serving

SERVES 4

FREEZE FOR UP TO 1 WEEK

1. Soak the preserved lemon in a bowl of cold water for 10 minutes to eliminate some of the saltiness. Soak the saffron strands in a cup with water. Drain the lemon and slice into thin rings, then halve each slice.

2. To make the dressing, mix the saffron strands (including the soaking water) with the olive oil, preserved lemon, and chile in a bowl. Mix the chicken, green beans, and dressing in a bowl. To serve without freezing, add the cilantro leaves. Serve with flatbread.

To freeze: Do not add the cilantro to the salad. Divide the salad between two 1-quart plastic freezer bags. Squeeze out as much air as possible and seal. Lay the bags flat in the freezer and freeze until solid, about 1 hour. Once the bags are solid, store more compactly in the freezer.

To thaw: Place the bags on a plate and thaw in the refrigerator for 6 hours or overnight.

To serve: Remove the bag of chicken salad from the refrigerator at least 20 minutes before required. Allow to return to room temperature. Mix in the cilantro leaves and serve.

Roasted Pumpkin Soup

When you make a double batch of soup, you can very easily alter the flavor of the one to be frozen so that it tastes completely different.

1 large or 2 small ripe pumpkins or
  butternut squash (at least 4
  pounds), halved, seeds removed

2 tablespoons vegetable oil

2 tablespoons unsalted butter

1 large onion

3 garlic cloves, mashed to a paste
  with 1/2 teaspoon sea salt flakes

1 quart chicken or vegetable stock

Salt and freshly ground black
  pepper

1/3 cup crème fraîche

MAKES 2 QUARTS

1. Preheat the oven to 350°F. Place a rack in the top third of the oven.

2. Place the pumpkin halves, cut side down, on a large baking sheet lined with parchment paper. Roast for 1 1/2 hours or until the pumpkin is very soft to the touch. It should not brown on the cut surface; if browning too quickly, reduce the oven temperature by 50°F. (Squash will roast much faster; check after 45 minutes.) Allow the pumpkin to cool slightly.

3. Heat the oil in a skillet over low heat. Add the butter and once foaming, add the onion and garlic and cook for 8 minutes or until soft but not browned. Place the onion mixture and the pumpkin in a blender and puree until smooth. You may need to add a little of the stock and process in two batches to help puree more efficiently. Transfer the puree to a large pot and add the remaining stock. Season with salt and pepper to taste. Bring to a boil and cook for 5 minutes.

4. Set aside half of the soup to make into Thai Pumpkin and Coconut Soup (page 68). Serve the remaining soup with the crème fraîche either stirred throughout or swirled into each individual bowl.

Thai Pumpin and Coconut Soup

2 tablespoons Thai red curry paste

One 15-ounce can unsweetened
coconut milk

Roasted Pumpkin Soup (page 66)

Juice of 1 to 2 limes

Bean sprouts and fresh cilantro
or Thai basil leaves for serving,
optional

MAKES 1 QUART

FREEZE FOR UP TO 2 WEEKS

Place the curry paste and coconut milk in a pot and cook, stirring, for 3 minutes. Add the pumpkin soup and lime juice and simmer for 5 to 8 minutes. Serve with bean sprouts and cilantro.

To freeze: Allow the soup to cool completely to room temperature, then freeze in two small 2-cup containers, leaving a $^3/_4$- to 1-inch space at the top. Alternatively, freeze in two 1-quart plastic freezer bags. Seal and freeze flat until solid, about 1 hour. Once solid, pack the bags more compactly in the freezer.

To thaw: If stored flat in bags, thaw for 1 hour immersed in a bowl of cold water at room temperature, or 4 hours in the fridge. If stored in plastic containers, thaw overnight in the fridge. The soup does not have to be completely defrosted before heating.

To serve: Place the thawed or partially thawed soup in a pot and bring to a boil; reduce the heat and simmer for 5 to 10 minutes until heated through. Serve with bean sprouts and cilantro.

Basic Tomato Sauce

Make this delicious simple sauce when there is an abundance of cherry or grape tomatoes. Serve on pasta or freeze as is and serve as a tomato soup topped with a gremolata. It can also be used to top Tomato and Ricotta Cannelloni (page 96).

MAKES 3 QUARTS

FREEZE FOR UP TO 1 MONTH

8 pounds cherry tomatoes or small
  plum tomatoes

¼ cup extra virgin olive oil

3 shallots, finely chopped

6 garlic cloves, crushed to a paste
  with 1 teaspoon sea salt flakes

4 large basil or rosemary sprigs

3 large flat-leaf parsley sprigs

Salt and freshly ground black
  pepper

2 teaspoons brown sugar, if
  necessary

1. Place the tomatoes in a large pot or Dutch oven with 6 tablespoons water. Dampen a large piece of crumpled parchment paper with cold water, open it, and place it directly over the tomatoes. Cover the pot and cook over very low heat for 30 minutes, shaking the pot occasionally to stir. Do not open, as the tomatoes are sweating and cooking in their own steam.

2. Transfer the tomatoes to a food processor, in two to three batches if necessary, and process until smooth. Strain through a sieve, discarding the skins and seeds. Place the tomatoes, olive oil, shallots, garlic, and herbs in a pot. Bring to a boil, reduce the heat, and simmer for 40 to 50 minutes until reduced to 12 cups. Season with salt and pepper to taste, adding the sugar if necessary.

To freeze: Allow the sauce to cool completely to room temperature, then divide among six 1-quart plastic freezer bags—each bag will contain about 2 cups of sauce, making each bag only about half full. Freeze flat until solid, about 1 hour. When solid, store more compactly in the freezer.

To thaw: Thaw the bags of sauce completely immersed in a bowl of cold water, about 1½ hours to partially thaw. Or put the bags of sauce on a plate and thaw in the refrigerator for about 4 hours. You do not have to completely thaw the sauce before you heat it.

To serve: Transfer the thawed sauce to a pot, bring to a boil, reduce the heat, and simmer for 5 minutes. If only partially thawed, simmer for an extra 5 minutes.

Tomato Soup with Gremolata

2 cups Basic Tomato Sauce

   (page 69), thawed if frozen

1 garlic clove, finely chopped

Finely grated zest of 1 lemon or

   half an orange

2 tablespoons finely chopped fresh

   flat-leaf parsley

1 to 2 tablespoons extra virgin

   olive oil

Crusty bread for serving

SERVES 2

1. Heat the thawed sauce as explained on page 70.

2. For the gremolata, mix the garlic, lemon zest, and parsley in a small bowl. Ladle the soup into two serving bowls, drizzle each with a little olive oil, then sprinkle the gremolata on top. Serve with crusty bread.

Amatriciana Pasta Sauce

1 pound bucatini pasta

1 tablespoon olive oil

2 tablespoons butter

1 small onion, finely chopped

One 4-ounce piece of pancetta,
cut into ¼-inch-thick short strips

1 fresh hot red chile, finely
chopped, or 1 teaspoon crushed
red pepper

2 cups Basic Tomato Sauce (page
69), thawed if frozen

Freshly grated pecorino and
freshly ground black pepper for
serving

SERVES 4

1. Bring a large pot of salted water to a boil. Add the pasta and return to a rolling boil. Cook for 10 to 12 minutes or until the pasta is al dente. Drain, reserving about 1 cup of the pasta water.

2. Meanwhile, heat the oil in a large skillet over medium heat. Add the butter and when foaming, add the onion and cook for 5 to 8 minutes until soft. Add the pancetta and chile and cook for 10 minutes. Stir in the tomato sauce and bring to a boil. Reduce the heat and simmer for 5 minutes.

3. Return the drained pasta to the pasta pot and add the sauce. Toss to mix, adding some of the reserved pasta water to thin, if needed. Serve immediately with the pecorino and black pepper.

Bolognese Sauce

This classic meat sauce gets its rich taste from slow cooking. Serve with tagliatelle pasta or use for Meat and Potato Pie (page 77). To serve with pasta, you will need 2 to 3 cups meat sauce to 1 pound dried tagliatelle; this will be enough to serve four. Serve with freshly grated Parmesan cheese.

2 tablespoons olive oil

2 tablespoons unsalted butter

1 large onion, finely chopped

3 celery stalks, chopped

1 large carrot, peeled and chopped

3 pounds ground beef chuck

Salt and freshly ground black
    pepper

2 cups whole milk

1 cup dry white wine

One 28-ounce can whole Italian
    plum tomatoes in juice, coarsely
    chopped

1 tablespoon tomato paste

Freshly grated Parmesan for
    serving

MAKES 6 CUPS

FREEZE FOR UP TO 6 WEEKS

1. Heat the oil in a large heavy pot or Dutch oven over medium heat. Add the butter and when foaming, add the onion, celery, and carrot and cook for 10 minutes or until soft but not browned. Increase the heat and add the ground beef and salt and pepper to taste. Cook for 15 minutes, stirring constantly to break up the lumps. Once the liquid has evaporated, continue to cook until the meat just begins to brown.

2. Add the milk and bring to a boil. Reduce to a simmer. Cook for about 45 minutes, stirring occasionally, until the milk has evaporated. Add the wine and cook for 15 minutes, stirring, until it has evaporated. Finally, add the tomatoes, tomato paste, and 1 cup water. Cook for 2 hours over very low heat with the pot partially covered, until the meat is very tender. Stir occasionally; you may find it necessary to add a little extra water if the sauce is sticking at the bottom of the pot. Taste and adjust the seasoning and cook for another 5 minutes. The sauce should be thick, with the oil separating on the surface. Allow the sauce to sit for at least 15 minutes before serving. Serve with Parmesan.

To freeze: Allow the Bolognese sauce to cool completely to room temperature, then divide among three 1-quart plastic freezer bags. Each will contain 2 cups of sauce. Seal, squeezing out as much air as possible, then place the bags flat in the freezer, spreading out the sauce. Freeze flat until solid, about $1\frac{1}{2}$ hours. Once solid, store the bags more compactly in the freezer.

To thaw: Place the bags on a plate and refrigerate for at least 4 hours or overnight.

To serve: Transfer the sauce to a pot and bring to a boil. Reduce the heat and simmer for 15 minutes. Add $\frac{1}{2}$ cup water if the mixture looks too thick and cook for an extra 5 minutes for excess liquid to evaporate. Serve with Parmesan.

Meat and Potato Pie

This pie can be made along with the Bolognese sauce when it is first made. Simply set aside 3 cups of meat sauce before using or freezing the remainder. This way the pie can be frozen as well.

1½ pounds waxy potatoes
  (such as Yukon Gold), peeled
  and thinly sliced

2 teaspoons chopped fresh
  thyme leaves

3 cups Bolognese Sauce (page 74)

2 tablespoons unsalted butter,
  melted

3 tablespoons freshly grated
  Parmesan

SERVES 4 TO 6

FREEZE FOR UP TO 3 WEEKS

1. If planning to bake immediately, preheat the oven to 375°F. Place a rack in the center of the oven. Prepare a water bath by filling a large bowl with cold water and ice.

2. Bring a large pot of salted water to a boil. Reduce to a simmer, add half the potato slices, and cook for 3 minutes; they should not be cooked through. Drain the potatoes and plunge into the water bath. Repeat with the remaining potatoes. Drain.

3. Mix the thyme into the Bolognese sauce with ½ cup water. Lightly brush a 2-quart, shallow ovenproof and freezer-safe baking dish with some melted butter. Spoon the Bolognese sauce into the container and level the surface. Arrange half of the potatoes over the sauce; brush with melted butter and sprinkle with Parmesan. Repeat.

4. To cook immediately, bake for 50 minutes or until the potatoes are golden brown and cooked through.

   To freeze: Do not bake the assembled pie. Place a sheet of freezer paper over the potatoes and cover with heavy-duty foil. Freeze.

   To cook: Preheat the oven to 350°F. Place a rack in the center of the oven. Remove the foil and freezer paper from the pie. Re-cover with parchment paper and foil. Bake for 45 minutes, remove covers, and bake for another 30 minutes until brown. Serve.

Caramelized Onion and Mushroom Sauce

This sauce can be served with pasta, grilled steak, or broiled chicken or fish. Or freeze and give it a completely different shape and form with puff pastry. To serve with pasta, allow 3 cups sauce for 1 pound dried pasta to serve four.

3 tablespoons olive oil

2 tablespoons unsalted butter

3 large sweet onions (about 2½ pounds), cut into ½-inch-thick wedges

1 tablespoon honey

¾ pound fresh shiitake mushrooms, trimmed and wiped clean

1 large portobello mushroom, trimmed and wiped clean

1 pound small white or cremini mushrooms, trimmed and wiped clean

2 tablespoons chopped fresh flat-leaf parsley

3 tablespoons chopped fresh thyme leaves

2 tablespoons chopped fresh marjoram

3 tablespoons crème fraîche

Salt and black pepper

MAKES 6 CUPS

FREEZE FOR UP TO 2 WEEKS

1. Heat 2 tablespoons of the olive oil in a large deep skillet over medium heat. Add half of the butter and when foaming, add the onions. Reduce the heat to low. Dampen a piece of crumpled parchment paper with water, then open it and place it directly over the onions. Cover the skillet and cook for 20 minutes. Uncover, remove the paper, add the honey, and stir to mix. Increase the heat to medium and cook the onions for another 20 minutes, stirring frequently until caramelized.

2. Thickly slice all the mushrooms. Heat the remaining oil in a separate skillet over medium heat. Add the remaining butter and when foaming, add the mushrooms and cook for 10 minutes or until golden brown, stirring frequently. Add the herbs and cook for another minute.

3. Add the caramelized onions and crème fraîche to the mushrooms. Mix well and season with salt and pepper to taste.

To freeze: Allow the sauce to cool to room temperature, then divide among three 1-quart plastic freezer bags. Each bag will contain 2 cups of sauce. Seal, squeezing out as much air as possible. Lay the bags flat in the freezer and freeze until solid, about $1\frac{1}{2}$ hours. Once solid, store more compactly in the freezer.

To thaw: Place the bags of sauce on a plate and allow to thaw in the refrigerator for at least 4 hours or overnight.

To serve: Transfer the completely thawed sauce into a clean pot and add about $\frac{1}{4}$ cup water or vegetable stock to thin the sauce a little. Bring to a boil, reduce the heat, and simmer for 5 minutes before serving.

Mushroom Pot Pie

This pie can be served as a vegetarian main course or as a side dish for stews. Ideally, make this pie with fresh Caramelized Onion and Mushroom Sauce (page 78) if you intend to freeze the pie. See page 133 for pointers on how to use puff pastry successfully every time.

1 pound puff pastry, thawed if
   frozen

3 cups Caramelized Mushroom and
   Onion Sauce (page 78)

1 egg yolk beaten with
   2 tablespoons milk

¼ teaspoon sea salt flakes

SERVES 6

FREEZE FOR UP TO 3 WEEKS

1. Roll out the pastry to ¼ inch thick; fold into thirds, then roll again. Do this twice more. Fold for a final time, then halve the pastry. Roll one piece of pastry into a 12 × 10-inch rectangle. Trim the edges, so that the rectangle is no smaller than 11 × 9 inches. Transfer to a large baking sheet. Spoon the cold mushroom filling into the center of the pastry, leaving a 1-inch border. Brush the border with cold water.

2. Roll out the second piece of pastry, finishing with a neat 11 × 9-inch rectangle. Lay the pastry over the mushroom filling and press the edges together. Trim the edges slightly to neaten; tap the cut edge with the blade of a small sharp knife to separate the layers of the pastry. Cut three to five slits across the top of the pie at slight diagonals. Refrigerate for 1 hour.

> *continued*

3. Preheat the oven to 450°F. Place the rack in the top third of the oven. Brush the top of the pie with the egg glaze and sprinkle with the salt flakes. Bake for 20 minutes. Reduce the heat to 375°F. Bake for another 40 minutes or until the surface of the pie is golden brown; check to make sure that the bottom is golden brown as well. Cool slightly to serve.

To freeze: Do not bake; once the pie has chilled in the refrigerator, remove it and brush with the egg glaze (do not add the salt flakes). Freeze directly on the baking sheet until solid, about 2 hours. Once the pie is solid, remove from the baking sheet and wrap in plastic freezer wrap, then with heavy-duty foil. Freeze.

To cook: Cook directly from the freezer. Preheat the oven to 450°F. Place the rack in the center of the oven. Remove the foil and plastic wrap from the pie and place on a baking sheet. Bake for 40 minutes. Reduce the oven temperature to 375°F, cover the pie loosely with foil, and bake for another 40 minutes or until well risen and golden brown all over.

Oven-Poached Salmon

Serve this simple poached salmon with a salad of boiled new potatoes mixed with cooked green beans, finely chopped red onion, and Dijon mustard vinaigrette. Cook extra salmon for leftovers to make Salmon Fish Cakes (page 84).

One 4-pound whole salmon, head
   removed, cleaned

Salt and freshly ground black
   pepper

1 small bulb fennel, thinly sliced

2 lemons, thinly sliced

Lemon wedges for serving

SERVES 4 TO 6 WITH LEFTOVERS

1. Preheat the oven to 425°F. Place a rack in the center of the oven. Place a flat rack in a large roasting pan.

2. Wash the salmon and pat dry with paper towels. Rub salt and pepper all over and inside the cavity. Lay the salmon on the rack in the roasting pan. Insert the fennel and lemon slices in the cavity of the salmon. Pour enough water in the roasting pan to come just below the rack. Dampen a large piece of crumpled parchment with water, open it, and place it directly over the fish. Cover with foil, securing well around the edge of the roasting pan.

3. Place the salmon in the oven and cook for 25 to 40 minutes until it is just cooked through. Test by inserting a metal skewer into the fish—if it goes through easily, the fish is ready. Using a fork, you can also expose a bit of the flesh to see if the flesh is opaque. Remove from the oven and allow to stand, covered, for 10 minutes. Transfer to a platter with lemon wedges and serve with a salad.

Salmon Fish Cakes

Serve these fish cakes with a tartar sauce made of ½ cup mayonnaise mixed with ½ cup crème fraîche, 2 tablespoons chopped capers, ¼ cup chopped gherkins, and 2 tablespoons chopped fresh flat-leaf parsley. For a complete meal, serve the cakes with garlic-sautéed green beans and a green salad.

1 pound baking potatoes such as
   russet, peeled and cut into large
   chunks

2 tablespoons butter

¼ cup milk

Sea salt flakes and freshly ground
   black pepper

1 bunch scallions, light green and
   white parts only, finely chopped

1 tablespoon Dijon mustard

3 tablespoons chopped fresh flat-
   leaf parsley

1½ pounds Oven-Poached Salmon
   (page 83)

1 to 2 tablespoons lemon juice

½ cup all-purpose flour

2 eggs, beaten

1 cup dried fine bread crumbs

MAKES 8

FREEZE FOR UP TO 4 WEEKS

1. Place the potatoes in a pot with salted water to cover. Bring to a boil, reduce the heat, and simmer for 15 minutes or until soft. Drain the potatoes and return to the pot and cook for 2 minutes or until all the liquid is evaporated. Add the butter and milk and mash over a gentle heat until the potatoes are semi-smooth. Remove from the heat. Season with salt and pepper to taste. Add the scallions, mustard, and parsley to the potato mixture. Flake the fish into large pieces and gently fold into the potatoes. Add the lemon juice according to taste and adjust the salt and pepper if necessary.

2. Shape into eight ½-cup patties or balls. Place on a baking sheet lined with plastic wrap. Chill for 45 minutes.

3. Place the flour, eggs, and bread crumbs in three separate shallow bowls. Dredge the fish cakes in flour, dusting off any excess. Coat with egg and then bread crumbs. Place on the baking sheet lined with plastic wrap and chill for 15 minutes.

4. Preheat the oven to 400°F if baking. Place a rack in the top third of the oven.

5. The fish cakes can be baked or sautéed. To bake, place on a baking sheet lined with parchment paper and brushed with oil. Bake for 20 minutes or until golden brown and heated through. To sauté, heat $\frac{1}{4}$ cup oil in a nonstick skillet and cook four fish cakes at a time, for 5 minutes on each side. Drain on paper towels before serving.

To freeze: Open freeze the uncooked fish cakes until solid, about 1 hour. Once frozen, wrap each with plastic freezer wrap, followed by a plastic freezer bag. Or use heat-seal plastic bags, placing 2 cakes in each bag. Return to the freezer.

To cook: Preheat the oven to 400°F. Place a rack in the center of the oven. Line a baking sheet with parchment paper, then brush with oil. Place the frozen fish cakes on the baking sheet. Bake for 30 minutes or until golden and heated through.

Rice

Leftover rice freezes into perfect single grains that can be made into dishes requiring cooked rice, such as Chinese Fried Rice (page 88), pilaf, and rice salad.

MAKES 8 CUPS

FREEZE FOR UP TO 2 WEEKS

2 cups jasmine, basmati, or long-grain rice

1 teaspoon salt

1. Place the rice in a large bowl and cover with water. Let soak for 30 minutes. If cooking long-grain rice, you do not have to soak it, but it will need rinsing. Drain the rice through a large sieve. Wash the rice again by allowing cold water to run through the rice until the water coming through the sieve is clear.

2. Place the rice in a 2-quart pot and add enough water to come ½ inch above the rice. Bring the water to a boil, stirring occasionally. Add the salt. Reduce the heat slightly, cover, and cook for 8 minutes for jasmine rice, 10 minutes for basmati and long-grain rice. Remove from the heat and let the rice stand for at least 10 minutes before removing the lid. Fluff with a fork to serve.

To freeze: Let the rice cool completely to room temperature. Spread the rice on a baking sheet; gently rub the rice with 1 to 2 teaspoons vegetable oil to separate the grains. Open freeze the rice for 30 minutes or until the grains are solid. Divide among three 1-quart plastic freezer bags. Each bag will contain 2 cups of rice. Seal, squeezing out as much air as possible. Freeze the bags of rice stacked flat.

To serve: Use the rice straight from the freezer. See the following pages for recipes using leftover rice.

Chinese Fried Rice

For Thai fried rice, the egg is actually cooked at the end of the stir-fry. Follow the recipe below starting with step 2. Once the shrimp has been added, make a well in the center of the pan. Then add a beaten egg with sesame oil into the middle. Cook egg until just set, then stir for 30 seconds. Serve immediately.

3 eggs

Sea salt flakes

2 teaspoons toasted sesame oil

¼ cup vegetable oil

2 cups frozen cooked jasmine or
    basmati rice

1 teaspoon finely chopped fresh
    ginger

1 small onion, finely chopped

3 ounces thick-cut bacon or slab
    bacon, diced

8 ounces medium shrimp, peeled
    and deveined

2 teaspoons rice wine

½ teaspoon sugar

1 to 2 tablespoons soy sauce

SERVES 2 AS A MAIN COURSE

1. Beat the eggs in a bowl with a pinch of salt and 1 teaspoon of the sesame oil. Preheat a wok over medium-high heat. Add a little of the vegetable oil and heat until just smoking. Pour one-third of the beaten eggs into the wok, swirling to thinly spread the eggs. Cook for 1 minute or until the eggs are lightly set yet still soft. Place the cooked eggs on a plate and set aside. Repeat, making two more omelets. Roll up each omelet and set aside.

2. Wipe the wok clean with a paper towel and add the remaining vegetable oil. Add the rice and stir-fry for 2 to 3 minutes until the rice is coated with oil and begins to become golden. Stir in the ginger and onion and cook for 1 minute. Add the bacon and cook for 2 minutes. Add the shrimp and cook for another 2 minutes or until they turn pink.

3. Add the rice wine, sugar, soy sauce, and remaining sesame oil and stir-fry for another 2 minutes or until the shrimp are cooked through. Thinly slice the omelet into rings and add to the fried rice. Cook for 1 minute and serve.

Brown Butter Rice

Serve as a side dish for grilled meats, fish, or vegetables.

4 tablespoons (½ stick) unsalted butter

1 to 2 fresh sage or rosemary sprigs, optional

4 cups frozen cooked long-grain or basmati rice

Salt and freshly ground black pepper

SERVES 4

1. Place the butter in a large skillet over low heat. Once the butter is foaming, add the herbs and cook for 2 to 3 minutes more until the butter becomes a nutty brown color. Discard the herbs.

2. Add the rice to the skillet, coating well with the butter. Dampen a piece of crumpled parchment paper with water, open it, and place it directly over the rice. Cover the skillet. Cook for 5 minutes or until the rice is completely heated through. Season with salt and pepper to taste. Serve.

Tamarind Rice and Chana Dal

Chana dal are small, halved chickpeas that look very much like yellow split peas. Widely used as a side dish on Indian menus, chana dal adds a touch of sweetness to the savory dish. To speed up cooking times, you can presoak the chana dal. Serve as a main course for vegetarians, accompanied with toasted pita or naan bread, a chopped tomato, cucumber, and yogurt salad.

2 tablespoons tamarind pulp

2 tablespoons vegetable oil

1 teaspoon black mustard seeds

10 fresh or frozen curry leaves

2 small dried red chiles

1 small onion, peeled and finely
   chopped

1 cup chana dal or yellow lentils,
   picked over

½ teaspoon ground coriander

½ teaspoon turmeric powder

2 cups vegetable or chicken stock

2 cups frozen cooked basmati or
   long-grain rice

Naan bread and yogurt for serving

SERVES 4 AS A MAIN COURSE

1. Place the tamarind in a small bowl and add ¼ cup hot water. Let stand for 5 minutes, then strain through a sieve, discarding the seeds.

2. Heat the oil in a wok or deep skillet over medium heat. Add the mustard seeds, curry leaves, and dried chiles. Cook for 1 minute or until the seeds start to pop. Add the onion and cook for 5 minutes or until soft. Add the chana dal, coriander, and turmeric, and cook for 3 minutes or until the chana dal are coated. Stir in the stock and tamarind. Bring to a boil and cook for 30 minutes or until quite tender.

3. Stir the rice into the dal. Taste and adjust the seasoning. Cook for 10 minutes or until the rice is heated through and the dal is quite thick but not dry. Serve with naan bread and yogurt.

Rice Salad

This salad has been adapted from the classic Middle Eastern fattoush salad, which is traditionally made with crisp lavash bread. Serve with grilled, broiled, or steamed fish or chicken breasts.

1 small red onion, finely chopped

4 garlic cloves, crushed to a paste

    with sea salt flakes

1/3 cup extra virgin olive oil

Juice of 2 lemons

2 tablespoons ground sumac

    (available in Middle Eastern

    groceries)

Salt and freshly ground black

    pepper

3 cups frozen or thawed cooked

    long-grain rice

2 celery stalks, trimmed and finely

    sliced

1 small thin cucumber, diced

2 ripe tomatoes, seeded and diced

1 cup tightly packed fresh small

    mint sprigs

1 cup tightly packed small fresh

    flat-parsley sprigs

1 cup tightly packed small fresh

    cilantro sprigs

SERVES 4 AS A SIDE DISH

Place the onion, garlic paste, oil, lemon juice, sumac, and salt and pepper to taste in a bowl and mix to combine. Add the rice and stir to mix. Add the celery, cucumber, tomatoes, and herbs and toss to coat. Allow the salad to stand at room temperature for about 30 minutes until the rice is thawed and all the flavors are well blended.

Crepes

Crepes can be served any time of the day fill them with soft cheese such as ricotta and chopped fruit for breakfast. Fill with saut ed mushrooms and serve for lunch with a salad (page 95), or serve alone sprinkled with confectioners   sugar and lemon juice. For a dramatic dessert, transform them into crepes suzette. Fold each crepe (allowing two per person) into quarters and pan-fry in sugar dissolved in butter until caramelized. Add some orange juice and let bubble to a syrup. Add a dash of brandy, heat up, and ignite to flamb for crepes suzette. Crepes are also good substitutes for pasta when it comes to making cannelloni or lasagne (see pages 96 and 123).

2 cups all-purpose flour

½ teaspoon salt

6 large eggs

1 tablespoon vegetable oil

1¼ cups milk

1¼ cups heavy cream

2 tablespoons fine salt

1 potato

4 tablespoons (½ stick) butter,

  melted

MAKES 24 CREPES

FREEZE FOR UP TO 1 MONTH

1. Sift the flour and salt into a large bowl. Make a well in the center. Beat together the eggs, oil, milk, and cream in a bowl. Gradually add the egg mixture to the center of the flour mixture, beating between additions, and slowly drawing the flour into the wet mixture. The batter should be smooth. Cover with plastic wrap and let stand for 1 hour at room temperature or in the fridge overnight.

2. If the batter was in the fridge, allow to stand at room temperature for 20 minutes before using. Heat an 8-inch cast iron crepe pan or skillet until hot. Add about 2 tablespoons fine salt and scrub over the hot pan with a big pad of paper towels to make the pan nonstick. Discard the hot salt and wipe the pan clean. (If you have a nonstick pan, do not do this.) Wash the potato and cut in half. Dip the cut side of the potato into the melted butter. Use it to spread the melted butter; it helps spread the butter thinly and does not burn like paper!

3. Add ¼ cup of the batter to the pan and quickly spread by swirling the pan. Cook for 2 minutes on each side, turning once. Using a long flat spatula, gently lift up the crepe and flip over. Repeat 23 times.

4. Layer the crepes between squares of waxed paper to store.

To freeze: Allow the crepes to cool completely to room temperature. Leave the pile of crepes as is between sheets of waxed paper, and wrap the whole pile of crepes with plastic freezer wrap, then with heavy-duty foil. Freeze.

To thaw: Remove as many frozen crepes as required and leave at room temperature until soft, about 1 hour.

To serve: To heat the crepes, remove the waxed paper, and pile directly on top of each other. Wrap in foil and place in an oven preheated to 400°F for 5 minutes or until heated through.

Crepes with Sautéed Mushrooms

Use freshly made or thawed crepes for this recipe. Serve immediately—do not freeze.

1 tablespoon extra virgin olive oil

1 tablespoon unsalted butter

1 shallot, finely chopped

1 garlic clove, finely chopped

1 pound mixed mushrooms such as
   morel, cremini, cèpes (porcini),
   or shiitake, wiped clean

¼ cup heavy cream

3 tablespoons snipped fresh chives

Salt and freshly ground black
   pepper

4 crepes, warmed if frozen

2 tablespoons freshly, finely grated
   Parmesan

SERVES 2

1. Heat the oil in a large skillet over low heat. Add the butter and when foaming, add the shallot and garlic and cook for 5 minutes or until the shallot is soft. Add the mushrooms, increase the heat to medium, and cook for 15 minutes or until the mushrooms are soft and all liquid has evaporated. Stir in the heavy cream and 2 tablespoons of the chives. Season with salt and pepper to taste. Allow to simmer for 2 minutes.

2. Spoon 2 to 3 tablespoons of the mushroom filling in the center of each crepe and fold into a square: bring the right side over the filling, then the bottom part over the filling, then the left side over the filling, finishing with the top part of the crepe to enclose the filling. Flip over so that the seams are on the underside. Set on a serving plate or platter. Spoon the remaining mushroom sauce over the filled crepes. Sprinkle with Parmesan and garnish with the remaining chives. Serve.

Tomato and Ricotta Cannelloni

If using fresh crepes and tomato sauce not yet frozen, then you can freeze this dish. Otherwise bake the cannelloni on the day it was assembled.

2 tablespoons unsalted butter

2 tablespoons chopped fresh sage
    leaves

10 ounces fresh ricotta

Salt and freshly ground black
    pepper

1½ cups Basic Tomato Sauce
    (page 69), thawed if frozen

8 crepes, thawed if frozen

8 ounces fresh mozzarella, drained
    and sliced

1 tablespoon extra virgin olive oil

SERVES 4

FREEZE FOR UP TO 2 WEEKS

1. Preheat the oven to 400°F.

2. Melt the butter in a skillet over medium heat. Add the sage and cook for 5 to 8 minutes until the sage is crisp and the butter is a nutty brown color. In a bowl, mix the ricotta with the sage butter and salt and pepper to taste.

3. Spread ½ cup of tomato sauce in the bottom of a 2-quart, shallow, ovenproof, freezer-safe baking dish. Using 2 tablespoons of the ricotta mixture per crepe, place the filling along the bottom third of the crepe and roll up. Lay the rolled-up crepe on the sauce. Repeat, filling eight cannelloni total. Spoon the remaining tomato sauce over the cannelloni and top with mozzarella slices. Sprinkle with pepper and drizzle with olive oil. Bake for 30 minutes or until the sauce is bubbling and the mozzarella is golden brown. Let stand for 5 minutes before serving.

To freeze: Do not bake the assembled dish. Freeze uncovered until the surface is solid. Place a piece of plastic wrap on the surface, then cover with heavy-duty foil. Return to the freezer.

To cook: Preheat the oven to 400°F. Place a rack in the center of the oven and place a baking sheet in the oven to preheat. Remove the foil and plastic wrap from the cannelloni and replace with parchment paper and foil. Place the cannelloni on the baking sheet and bake for 30 minutes. Remove the foil and parchment paper and bake for another 20 minutes or until the mozzarella is golden brown and the sauce is bubbling.

cooking for a crowd

What better way to feed a crowd than from a big pot of aromatic stew? All the recipes in this chapter take a little time to prepare and are cooked slowly to help develop their mellow flavors. With all of the preparation done ahead of time, you can focus on more important things, like your guests.

Since savory pies are also excellent one-pot dishes to serve to a crowd, consider the Smoked Paprika Steak Pie (page 151) or the Chicken and Leek Pot Pies (page154) when thinking of your menu.

Fresh pasta is exceptionally special and a treat for family and friends. Freeze the pasta assembled or freeze in sheets. Lasagne and pasta bakes freeze very well and make excellent one-pot meals to feed a crowd. Homemade ravioli cooks in minutes and draws praise and satisfaction.

Marsala Beef Stew

When purchasing meat for this recipe, look for chuck or stewing beef with a good amount of fat marbled throughout. Lean meat will result in a dry, tough stew. Serve the Mushroom Pot Pie (page 80) as the side dish.

2 pounds beef chuck, cut into
  1½-inch chunks

MARINADE

2 onions, coarsely chopped

2 celery stalks, sliced

2 large carrots, peeled, halved
  lengthwise, and cut into
  ½-inch-thick slices

3 garlic cloves, lightly smashed
  with skins intact

1 cup full-bodied red wine

2 tablespoons extra virgin olive oil

4 fresh thyme sprigs

4 fresh marjoram sprigs

SERVES 6

FREEZE FOR UP TO 2 MONTHS

1. Put the meat in a large plastic or glass container and add the onions, celery, carrots, and garlic. Add the red wine, oil, and herbs and toss to coat. Cover and let marinate in the refrigerator overnight.

2. Put the porcini in a bowl. Heat the Marsala until just boiling, then pour over the porcini. Cover and let soak for 45 minutes.

3. Remove the marinated meat and vegetables from the refrigerator and let drain in a sieve. Transfer the meat to a paper-towel-lined plate. Let drain for 5 minutes. Allow the vegetables to continue draining in the sieve. Discard the herbs.

4. Heat a large Dutch oven over medium-high heat. Add 2 tablespoons of the oil and sear the beef in one or two batches for 10 to 15 minutes, turning frequently, until browned all over and any excess liquid evaporates. Transfer the meat to a bowl and set aside. Add another 2 tablespoons of the oil, heat, and sear the second batch of meat. Transfer the additional meat to the bowl.

> *continued*

STEW

1 ounce dried porcini mushrooms

1 cup sweet Marsala

5 to 6 tablespoons olive oil

One 4-ounce piece slab bacon,
  cut into strips about ¼ inch
  wide, 1 inch long

2 cups full-bodied red wine

2 tablespoons tomato paste

3 to 4 cups beef stock

3 fresh thyme sprigs

3 fresh marjoram sprigs

2 bay leaves, preferably fresh

Salt and freshly ground black
  pepper

5. Add 1 tablespoon of the oil to the Dutch oven and fry the bacon for 8 minutes or until brown and crisp. Drain the bacon on a paper-towel-lined plate before adding to the bowl of meat.

6. If needed, add the remaining oil to the Dutch oven and stir in the vegetable mixture. Cook for 10 minutes or until the onions are soft and just beginning to brown. Transfer the vegetable mixture to the bowl containing the meat. Return the Dutch oven to the heat.

7. Preheat the oven to 350°F. Place a rack in the lower third of the oven. Add the wine to the Dutch oven and use a wooden spoon to scrape up any browned bits. Bring the mixture to a boil and cook for 5 minutes. Meanwhile, use a slotted spoon to transfer the porcini to a food processor. Strain the remaining Marsala through a paper-towel-lined fine sieve to remove any sediment. Add the strained Marsala and tomato paste to the food processor and puree until smooth. Add the puree to the Dutch oven. Add the meat and vegetable mixture to the wine mixture. Add 3 cups of the beef stock and bring to a boil. Add the herbs and season with salt and pepper to taste.

8. Dampen a piece of crumpled parchment paper with water, open it, and place it directly on the stew. Cover the pot with a tight-fitting lid and transfer to the oven. Cook for 3 hours or until the meat is very tender and almost falling apart. Add the final cup of stock when needed, if the stew is getting too thick. Discard the bay leaves. Taste and adjust the seasoning before serving.

To freeze: Allow the stew to cool completely to room temperature. Divide the stew into thirds and pack into three 2-quart plastic freezer bags. Seal, removing as much air as possible. Freeze flat until solid, about 2 hours. Stack in the freezer once solid.

To thaw: Place the bags on a plate and thaw in the refrigerator for 4 to 6 hours or overnight until the bag feels ice free.

To serve: Transfer the stew to a pot and add $\frac{1}{2}$ cup water. Dampen a piece of crumpled parchment paper with water, open it, and place it directly on the stew. Cover with a lid and gently heat over low heat for 20 minutes or until the stew is heated through and gently bubbling, stirring at least twice. Do not let the stew bubble too vigorously, as the meat will fall apart.

Coq au Vin

The richer flavor of dark chicken meat makes for the best stews and casseroles. The marinating part can be left out, although it does create a deeper flavor. Serve with mashed potatoes or tagliatelle and green beans.

If you have any coq au vin left over, remove the meat from the bones and return it to the sauce. Reheat and serve with pappardelle noodles. Do not freeze leftover chicken if the casserole was frozen beforehand. Store in the fridge for up to two days.

MARINADE

8 whole chicken legs

1 onion, coarsely chopped

3 garlic cloves, lightly smashed
   with skins intact

6 fresh thyme sprigs

3 fresh marjoram sprigs

1 cup dry white wine

¼ cup extra virgin olive oil

SERVES 8

FREEZE FOR UP TO 2 MONTHS

1. Place the chicken in a large plastic or glass container with the onion, garlic, and herbs. Add the wine and oil and rub into the chicken. Cover and let marinate for 4 hours or overnight in the fridge.

2. Remove the chicken from the refrigerator. Use a slotted spoon to transfer the chicken to a paper-towel-lined plate. Pat dry and let sit for 10 minutes. Discard all the remaining marinade ingredients.

3. To prepare the stew, heat 2 tablespoons of the oil in a large Dutch oven over medium heat. Add the bacon and cook for about 10 minutes, until brown and crisp. Transfer to a paper-towel-lined plate and set aside.

4. Place the flour in a shallow bowl and season with salt and pepper. Add 2 tablespoons of the butter to the Dutch oven, and once foaming, lightly dredge half of the chicken with the seasoned flour and add to the pot. Cook for 10 minutes, turning frequently, until golden brown. Transfer to a paper-towel-lined plate. Add another tablespoon of the oil for the second batch of chicken and cook for an additional 10 minutes. Transfer to the paper-towel-lined plate and return the Dutch oven to the heat.

> *continued*

STEW

¼ cup olive oil

One 6-ounce piece slab bacon, cut
into strips about ¼ inch wide
and 1 inch long

2 tablespoons all-purpose flour

Salt and freshly ground black
pepper

4 tablespoons (½ stick) unsalted
butter

3 cups medium-bodied red wine

½ cup sweet Marsala

2 cups chicken stock

1 pound pearl onions, peeled but
left whole

8 ounces cremini mushrooms,
wiped clean and trimmed

3 tablespoons chopped fresh
thyme leaves

1 tablespoon chopped fresh
marjoram leaves

5. Preheat the oven to 350°F. Place a rack in the lower third of the oven.

6. Add the red wine to the Dutch oven and increase the heat to high. Bring to a boil and use a wooden spoon to scrape up any browned bits. Boil for 10 minutes. Place the chicken and bacon in the Dutch oven and add the Marsala and stock. Bring to a boil. Dampen a piece of crumpled parchment paper with water, open it, and place it directly on the casserole. Cover the pot tightly with a lid and transfer to the oven. Cook for 1½ hours.

7. Heat the remaining oil in a skillet over medium heat. Add the remaining butter, and once foaming, add the pearl onions and mushrooms and cook for 10 minutes or until golden brown. Add the herbs and cook for another minute or two. Transfer the mixture to the Dutch oven. Return the pot to the oven and cook for another 30 minutes. Either serve on the day of making or cool and chill for the next day.

To freeze: Allow the chicken and juices to cool completely to room temperature. Pack no more than two portions per 1-quart freezer bag, including vegetables and juices. Seal, removing as much air as possible. Freeze flat until solid, about 2 hours. Stack in the freezer once solid.

To thaw: Place the bags of the chicken on a plate and thaw in the refrigerator for 6 hours or overnight. The chicken and juices should be ice free.

To serve: Transfer the coq au vin to a shallow casserole dish and add ½ cup water. Dampen a piece of crumpled parchment paper with water, open it, and place directly over the stew. Cover the dish with a tight-fitting lid. Cook in an oven preheated to 375°F for 30 minutes or until heated through and the juices start to bubble. Serve.

Mexican Chickpea Stew with Green Salsa

Keep the atmosphere very buffet style and relaxed with this Mexican pozole soup-stew. All the hard work will be done and you just need to deal with the accompaniments on the day of serving. Serve with sliced cucumbers, radishes, limes, and extra jalapeño chiles; dice an avocado or two; chop and mix chipotle chiles in adobo sauce with sour cream; shred some cheese and romaine lettuce; select and wash a bunch of fresh cilantro sprigs; pile tortilla chips in a bowl. Invite your guests to add as much or as little of the accompaniments to their stews as they like.

If you want to cook your own chickpeas, soak 1½ cups dried chickpeas in water overnight. Drain and wash. Place in a pot of cold water. Add a chopped onion and 2 chopped celery stalks. Cook for 2 hours or until the chickpeas are tender. Drain and reserve the cooking liquid to use in place of stock.

½ cup pepitas (hulled green pumpkin seeds)

2 poblano chiles

1½ pounds tomatillos, husked and washed

2 fresh jalapeño chiles

1 cup tightly packed fresh cilantro leaves, coarsely chopped

1 teaspoon Mexican oregano

Salt and freshly ground black pepper

2 tablespoons vegetable oil

1 large white onion, roughly chopped

1 quart vegetable stock

1. Toast the pepitas in a large dry skillet until puffed but not browned, about 3 minutes. Cool slightly, then place in a spice grinder and grind until a fine powder has formed. Set aside.

2. Char-grill the poblanos over an open gas flame until the skin is blackened. Alternatively, rub with a little oil and roast in an oven preheated to 400°F for 20 minutes until the skins blister and brown. The skins will not blacken in the oven. Place the chiles in a bowl, cover with plastic wrap, and let cool.

3. Heat a large grill pan over high heat. Add the tomatillos and jalapeños and cook until the skins are blackened, about 20 minutes. Scrape the skins from the poblanos and discard the seeds, core, and stems. Do not remove the skins or seeds from the tomatillos or jalapeños.

> *continued*

Two 15-ounce cans white hominy,

rinsed and drained

Two 15-ounce cans chickpeas,

rinsed and drained

1 pound Swiss chard, washed, tough

stems discarded, cut into strips

Juice from 2 limes

SERVES 8

FREEZE FOR UP TO 4 WEEKS

4. To make the green salsa, place the poblanos, tomatillos, jalapeños, $\frac{1}{2}$ cup of the cilantro, the oregano, and salt and pepper to taste in a food processor. Process to a puree and set aside.

5. To prepare the stew, heat the oil in a large pot over medium heat. Add the onion and cook for 5 minutes or until soft. Stir in the green salsa and cook for 10 minutes, stirring frequently, until thickened. Stir in the ground pepitas and 1 cup of the vegetable stock. Bring to a boil, reduce the heat, and allow to simmer for 5 minutes. Add the remaining stock, the hominy, and chickpeas. Bring to a boil, reduce the heat, and simmer for 15 minutes.

6. Add the Swiss chard to the stew and simmer for another 15 minutes. If not intending to freeze, adjust the seasoning and stir in the lime juice to taste with the remaining cilantro. Serve with accompaniments.

To freeze: Do not add the lime juice or cilantro. Allow the stew to cool completely to room temperature. Divide into thirds and transfer to three 1-quart plastic freezer bags. Seal, removing as much air as possible. Freeze flat until solid, about 2 hours. Stack in the freezer once solid.

To thaw: Place the bags on a plate; thaw in the refrigerator for 4 hours or overnight until soft and ice free.

To serve: Transfer the stew to a pot, add $\frac{1}{4}$ cup water per bag, and simmer over low heat for 10 minutes or until heated through. Add the lime juice and cilantro before serving.

To serve from frozen: Transfer the solid stew to a large pot, adding $\frac{1}{4}$ cup water per bag. Cover and simmer very slowly over low heat, stirring occasionally until heated through, about 30 minutes. Add the cilantro and lime juice just prior to serving.

Seafood Pie

The topping for this pie is a celeriac puree mixed with potatoes; vegetable purees freeze extremely well. Celeriac is a root vegetable recognized by its knobby, light brown bulbous appearance. As the name suggests, its flavor is very similar to that of celery, but sweeter. During the winter months, celeriac has a white flesh that turns golden yellow in the summer. Serve this savory pie for brunch or lunch with a simple watercress salad dressed with lemon juice and olive oil.

1½ cups milk

2 large fresh flat-leaf parsley sprigs

½ small onion, cut into wedges

2 garlic cloves, lightly smashed

1 pound boneless monkfish fillet,
   cut into 1½-inch chunks

12 ounces sea scallops, halved or
   quartered, depending on size

1 pound peeled and deveined
   small shrimp

8 ounces smoked trout fillets

2 tablespoons unsalted butter

¼ cup all-purpose flour

2 tablespoons crème fraîche

2 tablespoons Dijon mustard

2 tablespoons capers, soaked in hot
   water for 10 minutes, then drained

Sea salt flakes and freshly ground
   black pepper

SERVES 6

FREEZE FOR UP TO 2 WEEKS

1. Place the milk, parsley, onion, and garlic in a deep skillet and bring to a boil. Add the monkfish, cover, and cook for 5 minutes. Add the scallops and shrimp, cover, and return to a boil. Remove from the heat and let stand for 10 minutes, covered.

2. Use a slotted spoon to gently lift the seafood from the milk and place in a large bowl. Flake the smoked trout into large pieces, discarding the skin and bones, and add the trout to the bowl of seafood.

3. Strain the milk through a paper-towel-lined sieve and set aside. Melt the butter in a clean pot over medium heat. Stir in the flour and cook for 2 minutes, stirring constantly. Remove from the heat and gradually whisk in the reserved milk. Return to the heat and cook for 5 minutes, stirring constantly until thick. Remove from the heat and stir in the crème fraîche, mustard, and capers. Allow the sauce to cool slightly, then gently fold into the seafood mixture. Season with salt and pepper to taste. Cover the surface directly with plastic wrap to prevent a skin from forming.

> *continued*

1½ pounds celeriac, peeled and
cut into 1-inch chunks

1½ pounds baking potatoes such
as russet, peeled and cut into
1-inch chunks

1 tablespoon unsalted butter

½ cup crème fraîche

Salt and freshly ground black
pepper to taste

4. To prepare the topping, place the celeriac in a pan of salted water. Bring to a boil, reduce the heat slightly, and cook for 20 minutes or until tender. At the same time, cook the potatoes in a separate pot of boiling salted water for 20 minutes or until tender. Drain the celeriac and puree in a food processor. Drain the potatoes and return to the pot. Cook over low heat for 2 minutes to evaporate any liquid. Add the butter and mash with a potato masher. Stir in the pureed celeriac, crème fraîche, and salt and pepper to taste. Stir the mixture until it is smooth and holds its shape.

5. Preheat the oven to 400°F. Place a rack in the center of the oven.

6. Spoon the seafood mixture into a 9 × 13 freezer-safe baking dish. Using two spoons of the same size, make ovals with the vegetable puree and place evenly over the fish mixture, leaving some spaces here and there, which is very important if the pie is to be frozen. The spaces will allow the food to thaw more quickly and evenly.

7. Place the pie on a large baking sheet and bake for 40 minutes or until the topping is golden brown and the filling is bubbling. Let stand for 10 minutes before serving.

To freeze: Do not bake once the pie is assembled. Allow to cool completely to room temperature. Place the pie, uncovered, in the freezer until solid, about 3 hours. Cover the surface with plastic freezer wrap, then heavy-duty foil. Freeze.

To thaw: Remove the pie from the freezer and remove the foil and plastic wrap. Loosely drape the surface with clean plastic wrap. Place the pie in the refrigerator and allow to thaw overnight.

To cook: Preheat the oven to 400°F and place a baking sheet in the oven to preheat. Place the pie on the baking sheet and loosely cover with foil. Bake for 50 minutes or until the sauce is bubbling and the top is golden brown. To check if the pie has heated through, insert the blade of a small knife into the center of the pie. If the blade feels hot, the pie is ready. Allow to cool slightly before serving.

Osso Buco Milanese Style

The traditional accompaniment to osso buco is a saffron risotto, Milanese style. I prefer a dish that can be made ahead such as a buttery Parmesan polenta, creamy mashed potatoes, or big pappardelle noodles to absorb all the hearty juices.

¼ cup olive oil

2 tablespoons unsalted butter

1 large onion, finely chopped

1 celery heart, trimmed and finely
   diced

2 large carrots, peeled and finely
   diced

2 garlic cloves, finely chopped

2 long strips lemon zest

3 tablespoons all-purpose flour

Salt and freshly ground black pepper

8 veal shanks, 1½ inches thick and
   at least 2 inches wide (each
   about 8 ounces)

1 cup dry white wine

2 cups veal or beef stock

One 15-ounce can whole Italian
   plum tomatoes in juice, coarsely
   chopped

3 fresh thyme sprigs

1 bay leaf, preferably fresh

3 fresh flat-leaf parsley sprigs

SERVES 8

FREEZE FOR UP TO 2 MONTHS

1. Choose an ovenproof pot large enough to accommodate all the veal shanks in one layer. Heat 1 tablespoon of the oil over medium heat. Add the butter and when foaming, add the onion, celery, and carrots. Cook for 10 minutes or until soft. Stir in the garlic and lemon zest and cook for another 2 minutes. Remove the pot from the heat and set aside.

2. Place the flour in a shallow bowl and season with salt and pepper. Pat the veal shanks dry; make sure they are securely tied around the middle of the circumference with kitchen twine. Heat 2 tablespoons of the oil in a large skillet over medium heat. Dredge four veal shanks with seasoned flour and place in the skillet. Brown the shanks on all sides, about 15 minutes altogether. Place the shanks in the pot with the sautéed vegetables. Add the remaining oil to the skillet and brown the remaining dredged shanks. Transfer the remaining shanks to the pot with the vegetables. Return the skillet to the heat.

3. Preheat the oven to 350°F. Place a rack in the lower third of the oven.

> *continued*

GREMOLATA

2 teaspoons grated lemon zest

½ teaspoon finely chopped garlic

2 tablespoons finely chopped fresh
   flat-leaf parsley

4. Add the wine to the skillet and cook for 2 minutes, scraping up any browned bits with a wooden spoon. Add the stock, tomatoes, and herbs to the skillet. Season with salt and pepper to taste. Bring the mixture to a boil. Pour the contents of the skillet over the veal shanks. Return the large pot to the stove and bring to a boil.

5. Dampen a piece of crumpled parchment paper with water, open it, and place it directly on the osso buco. Cover the pot with a tight-fitting lid and transfer to the oven. Cook for 2½ hours, basting and turning the meat every 45 minutes. If the liquid starts to look insufficient toward the end, add 2 tablespoons water when needed. The meat should be falling off the bone when pierced with a fork.

6. Mix the gremolata ingredients together and sprinkle over each shank 2 minutes before removing from the oven. Allow to stand for 10 minutes before serving.

To freeze: Stop cooking the osso buco after 2 hours if it is to be frozen and do not add the gremolata. Remove from the oven and allow to cool completely. Transfer two veal shanks and some juices and vegetables to each of four 2-quart plastic freezer bags. Seal, extracting as much as air as possible. Freeze flat until solid. Arrange in the freezer.

To thaw: Place the bags of osso buco on a plate. Thaw in the refrigerator overnight until soft and ice free.

To serve: Preheat the oven to 350°F. Transfer the thawed osso buco to a large ovenproof pot and sprinkle with ½ cup water. Dampen a piece of crumpled parchment paper with water, open it, and place directly over the osso buco; cover the pot with a tight-fitting lid. Bake for 40 minutes, turning the meat halfway through, until heated through. Add the gremolata 2 minutes before removing from the oven.

successful
slow cooking

The secret to successful stews, casseroles, and braises is to keep the surface of the stew or casserole directly covered at all times during cooking with a dampened crumpled piece of parchment paper. This helps to keep the moisture and steam circulating throughout the stew, rather than being lost in the space between the lid and the ingredients, sometimes causing meat to dry out. Using this parchment method will yield perfect results every time.

homemade pasta

Making homemade pasta requires a pasta machine. The advantage of using the freezer for fresh rolled-out pasta is that it can be placed in the freezer immediately and it will not stick together. Simply roll out the pasta, fill and shape ravioli, then freeze immediately. Cook straight from the freezer.

Allow three ravioli per person as an appetizer or five to six ravioli per main course. Follow the main course with a simple salad of radicchio, toasted pine nuts, and capers, tossed with a dressing of red wine vinegar and extra virgin olive oil, Dijon mustard, honey, and salt and pepper.

Lamb Ragù Ravioli
with Rosemary Brown Butter

FILLING

1 pound lamb shoulder, cut into
  1½-inch chunks

Salt and freshly ground black
  pepper

2 tablespoons olive oil

1 large onion, roughly chopped

2 celery stalks, chopped

1 cup full-bodied red wine

¾ cup canned whole Italian plum
  tomatoes and juice, chopped

2 tablespoons chopped mixed
  fresh thyme and rosemary leaves

MAKES 32 RAVIOLI

FREEZE FOR UP TO 2 WEEKS

1. Preheat the oven to 400°F. Place a rack in the middle of the oven.

2. Season the lamb with salt and pepper. Heat the oil in a Dutch oven over high heat. Add the lamb and sear for 10 minutes on all sides until browned. Transfer to a paper-towel-lined plate. Spoon out all but 1 tablespoon fat from the pan. Reduce the heat to medium-low and add the onion and celery. Cook for 8 to 10 minutes until soft and the onion begins to brown. Add the wine to the pot, increase the heat, and use a wooden spoon to scrape up any browned bits. Return the meat to the pot. Add the tomatoes and herbs and bring to a boil. Dampen a piece of crumpled parchment paper with water, open it, and place it directly over the meat. Cover the pot with a tight-fitting lid. Transfer to the oven and cook for 1 hour or until the meat is fork tender. Allow the filling to cool completely to room temperature. You may refrigerate it overnight if you prefer.

3. To prepare the pasta dough, sift the flour and salt into a food processor. Add the oil and process for 30 seconds or until the mixture resembles fine meal. Beat the whole eggs with the egg yolks in a small bowl. Gradually add the egg mixture to the flour mixture, pulsing between additions. Once the eggs have been added, pulse until the mixture comes together.

> *continued*

PASTA DOUGH

2 cups all-purpose flour

1 teaspoon fine salt

2 tablespoons olive oil

3 large eggs

2 large egg yolks

BROWN BUTTER

1 tablespoon olive oil

3 tablespoons unsalted butter

1 to 2 teaspoons crushed red
   pepper

2 large fresh rosemary sprigs,
   tough stalks removed but kept
   in small sprigs

6 tablespoons freshly grated
   pecorino

4. Sprinkle a clean surface with a little flour and turn out the dough. Knead for 10 minutes. The dough should become softer after about 8 minutes. Alternatively, you may use a standing mixer fitted with a dough hook to knead the dough, for 8 to 10 minutes. Wrap the pasta dough in plastic wrap and chill for a minimum of 1 hour and up to 24 hours.

5. Spoon off and discard any fat from the cooled lamb stew. Place the lamb mixture in a food processor and pulse until the meat is shredded and the juices are mixed together. Taste and adjust the seasoning. Set aside. Line two large baking sheets with plastic wrap and place in the freezer. Attach a pasta machine to your work surface.

6. Remove the pasta dough from the refrigerator and divide into four equal parts. Keep any dough you are not using draped with plastic wrap at all times to prevent it from drying out. Roughly stretch out one piece of dough and coat well with flour. Set your pasta machine on #1 to start. Feed the dough through twice. Move the setting to #2 and put the dough through once, making sure to keep the dough lightly coated with flour. Once the dough has gone through settings #3, #4, and #5, halve the dough crosswise and set half aside.

   Set the machine on #6 and feed the dough through once more—it will be almost paper thin. Allow the first half-piece of dough to rest while you put the second half-piece through. Put the first strip through once more and let rest—you will notice that it shrinks, so resting it is quite important. Repeat with the second strip of pasta. Shape each batch of rolled pasta into ravioli before putting another quarter of dough through the pasta machine.

> *continued*

7. Divide the strips of rolled-out dough into 4-inch squares (they do not need to be perfect). Working with one ravioli at a time, place a heaping teaspoon of filling in the center of a square, brush the edges with water, then fold into a triangle and press down gently on the sides to seal. Use a paring knife to trim the edges to neaten. Place on baking sheets in the freezer. Repeat with the remaining pasta dough until you have at least 32 ravioli.

8. If you want to serve the ravioli immediately, bring a large pot of water to a boil. Add 8 to 12 semi-frozen ravioli at a time. Return to a boil and cook for 2 minutes once the ravioli rises to the surface. Using a large, flat slotted spoon, remove the ravioli and place on a paper-towel-lined baking sheet to drain. Repeat with the remaining ravioli.

9. To prepare the brown butter sauce, heat the oil in a large skillet over medium heat. Add the butter and when foaming, add the red pepper and rosemary. Cook just until the butter turns brown, 2 to 3 minutes.

10. Add the drained ravioli in a single layer (you may need to do this in two batches) to the butter and cook for 1 minute on each side or until golden brown. Spoon the ravioli onto a large serving platter and sprinkle with pecorino. Continue cooking the remaining ravioli in the butter. The ravioli can be piled on top of one another. Serve with extra pecorino.

To freeze: Do not cook the ravioli. Open freeze the filled ravioli until solid, about 1 hour. Pack into plastic freezer bags and seal, squeezing out as much air as possible. Freeze flat, or pack into plastic containers once frozen solid.

To cook: Cook the ravioli straight from the freezer; boil the ravioli for 3 minutes instead of 2 minutes when they rise to the surface of the boiling water. Serve as on the previous page.

Lasagne

Your options here are endless. If you are making the lasagne to freeze, then make sure your sauces are all freshly made—choose from the Bolognese Sauce (page 74), Caramelized Onion and Mushroom Sauce (page 78), or the lamb filling used for the ravioli (page 118).

The prepared lasagne sheets can be frozen for up to 3 weeks. Wrap in plastic freeze wrap, then in plastic freezer-safe containers. Use straight from the freezer.

Half quantity of Fresh Pasta Dough (page 121)

3 cups milk

7 tablespoons butter

4½ tablespoons all-purpose flour

¼ teaspoon sea salt flakes or more to taste

3 cups Bolognese Sauce (page 74), Caramelized Onion and Mushroom Sauce (page 78), or Lamb Ragù (page 118)

1 cup finely grated Parmesan

SERVES 8

FREEZE FOR UP TO 4 WEEKS

1. Once the pasta dough is made, you will want to make sure that it rests for at least 1 hour in the refrigerator, so start by lining a baking sheet with plastic wrap and place in the freezer to chill. Remove the pasta dough from the refrigerator and divide into four equal parts. Keep any dough you are not using draped with plastic wrap at all times to prevent it from drying out. Roughly stretch out one piece of dough and coat well with flour. Set your pasta machine on #1 to start. Feed the dough through twice. Move the setting to #2 and put the dough through once, making sure to keep the dough lightly coated with flour. Once the dough has gone through settings #3, #4, and #5, halve the dough crosswise and set half aside. Set the machine on #6 and feed the first half piece through once more—it will be almost paper thin. Allow the first half-piece of dough to rest while you put the second half-piece through. Put the first strip through once more and let rest—you will notice that it shrinks, so resting it is quite important. Repeat with the second strip of pasta. Cut the sheets of pasta into 3 × 5-inch strips. Place the rectangles of pasta on the prepared baking sheet in the freezer. On top of the first layer, place another piece of plastic wrap followed by lasagne sheets. Continue until all the pasta dough is rolled out and cut into lasagne strips.

> *continued*

2. Bring a large pot of salted water to a boil. Fill a large bowl with cold water and add ice cubes. Gradually cook the pasta strips, directly from the freezer, about four at a time, for 2 minutes. Do not cook all the way through. Remove with a slotted spoon and place in the ice cold water. Leave for 1 minute, then drain on a baking sheet lined with paper towels.

3. To make the béchamel sauce, heat the milk in a pot to just below the boiling point. Transfer to a pitcher. Wipe out the pot and use it to melt 6 tablespoons of the butter. Once the butter is foaming, add the flour and beat well over medium heat for 2 minutes. Reduce the heat to low and gradually whisk in the warm milk. Season with salt. Increase the heat to medium and continue to cook and whisk the sauce until it comes to a boil. Cook for 2 minutes. Remove from the heat.

4. Preheat the oven to 400°F. Place a rack in the top third of the oven. Place a baking sheet in the oven to preheat.

5. Make sure your filling sauce or ragù is warm if previously frozen. Smear the remaining butter all over a 9 × 13-inch baking dish, at least 3 inches deep. Roughly spread 1 to 2 tablespoons of béchamel sauce on the bottom. Line the bottom with lasagne sheets, cutting to fit in the corners; do not overlap too much. Roughly spread with ½ cup sauce, followed with ½ cup béchamel sauce. Sprinkle with 2 tablespoons of the Parmesan. Top with lasagne sheets. Continue to make six layers of pasta (fresh pasta allows you to have this many layers!). Finish with the lasagne sheets, béchamel, and Parmesan.

6. Put the lasagne on the preheated baking sheet. Bake for 20 minutes or until a light crust forms at the top and the sauce is gently bubbling. Allow to rest for 10 minutes before serving.

To freeze: Freeze the unbaked, assembled lasagne uncovered until solid, about 2 hours. Place a piece of plastic freezer wrap directly on the surface, followed by heavy-duty foil. Freeze.

To thaw: Remove the foil and plastic freezer wrap and partially thaw in the refrigerator overnight until you can just pierce with a knife.

To bake: Preheat the oven to 350°F. Place a rack in the center of the oven and add a baking sheet to preheat. Place the lasagne on the baking sheet; cover with foil, and bake for 1 hour and 10 minutes. Remove the foil and bake for an additional 20 minutes or until the sauce is bubbling and the top is golden. Allow to rest for 10 minutes before serving.

Lamb Shanks and Preserved Lemon Tagine

This rich Moroccan stew is excellent served with its native couscous. Plain boiled potatoes tossed with olive oil, lemon juice, and chopped fresh parsley also make a perfect accompaniment for the assertive spices in the tagine.

There is no need to use the traditional tagine cooking vessel—the Dutch oven works wonders every time.

½ teaspoon ground cumin

½ teaspoon ground turmeric

½ teaspoon ground coriander

½ teaspoon cayenne pepper

1 tablespoon olive oil

2 tablespoons unsalted butter

Six ³/₄- to 1-pound lamb shanks

2 onions, coarsely chopped

2 garlic cloves, halved

1 cinnamon stick, halved

1 preserved lemon, finely chopped
    (see Glossary)

1 teaspoon saffron strands

2 cups lamb or vegetable stock

2 tablespoons honey

1 cup cracked green olives, pits
    removed

Salt and freshly ground black
    pepper

2 cups coarsely chopped fresh
    cilantro

1. Preheat the oven to 350°F. Place a rack in the lower third of the oven.

2. Mix all the spices together. Heat the oil in a large Dutch oven. Add the butter and when foaming, add the spices and cook for 1 minute. Add the lamb shanks, in batches, and cook for 5 minutes or until the meat is coated with the spices (do not worry about browning). Remove the lamb shanks and set aside.

3. Add the onions and garlic to the pot and cook for 5 minutes or until soft. Add the cinnamon stick, lemon, and saffron and cook for 2 minutes. Add the stock and honey. Bring to a boil and return the lamb shanks to the pot. Dampen a piece of crumpled parchment paper with water, open it, and place directly over the meat. Cover the pot with a tight-fitting lid. Transfer to the oven and cook for 3 hours or until the lamb is completely tender. Add the olives and season with salt and pepper to taste (do not season earlier, as the lemons and olives will determine the amount of salt needed).

SERVES 6

FREEZE FOR UP TO 6 WEEKS

4. Transfer the lamb shanks to a platter and keep warm. Reduce the pan juices over high heat for 20 minutes or until the juices are thickened and reduced to about 1½ cups. Stir in the cilantro and serve.

To freeze: Do not reduce the cooking liquid or stir in the cilantro. Allow the tagine to cool completely to room temperature, then place in the refrigerator for the fat to set on the surface, about 2 hours. Spoon off the top layer of fat and discard. Divide the lamb shanks and juices among three 2-quart plastic freezer bags. Seal, removing as much air as possible. Freeze flat until solid, about 2½ hours. Rearrange in the freezer once solid.

To thaw: Place the bags of tagine on a plate. Thaw in the refrigerator overnight until soft and ice free.

To serve: Preheat the oven to 375°F. Place the contents of the bags in a large ovenproof pot. Dampen a piece of crumpled parchment paper with water, open it, and place directly over the meat. Cover the pot with a tight-fitting lid. Cook for 30 minutes or until the meat is heated all the way through and the juices are bubbling. Stir in the cilantro and serve. You do not need to reduce the cooking liquid, as the removing of fat and freezing have eliminated any extra liquid.

Rabbit Stiffado

This dish is inspired by my mother's Greek method of cooking game—rabbit or pheasant with onions and vinegar served with lots of runny juices. The sweet onions and rich flavor from the game is cut with the simple addition of vinegar . . . I use sherry or wine vinegar; my mother uses any brown vinegar! Serve with nutty-tasting Brown Butter Rice (page 90) or lots of crusty bread to soak up the juices. If you're fortunate enough to have any left over, pull the meat from the bones and return to the sauce to serve with rigatoni pasta later on in the week.

14 ounces white pearl onions

2½ to 3 pounds rabbit or pheasant,
    cut into 8 serving pieces

Salt and freshly ground black
    pepper

¼ cup olive oil

4 to 5 ounces slab prosciutto, cut
    into ¼-inch dice

6 garlic cloves, peeled and kept
    whole

1 cup dry sherry

1 cup dry white wine

1 quart chicken stock

Small bouquet of fresh thyme,
    flat-leaf parsley sprigs,
    and 1 bay leaf

2 tablespoons good sherry vinegar
    or red wine vinegar

SERVES 6

FREEZE FOR UP TO 3 WEEKS

1. Peeling pearl onions is pretty boring; the fastest way I know is to blanch them for 1 minute, drain, and cool under cold water. Drain again. Using a small vegetable knife, peel the onions, leaving the roots intact. Set aside.

2. Season the rabbit with salt and pepper, rubbing well into the meat. Heat the oil in a large Dutch oven. Brown the meat all over, about 10 minutes; you may need to do this in batches. Remove the meat and drain on a paper-towel-lined plate; set aside.

3. Preheat the oven to 350°F. Set a rack in the center of the oven.

4. There should be 1 to 2 tablespoons oil left in the pot; if not, add a little more. Stir in the onions and prosciutto; cook for 10 minutes or until coated with oil and the onions just begin to soften. Stir in the garlic cloves. Pour the sherry over the onions and stir to deglaze the pot; cook for 2 minutes. Add the wine and bring to a boil. Cook for 5 minutes.

5. Return the rabbit to the pot and add enough stock to just cover the meat. Add the herbs and bring to a boil. Dampen a piece of crumpled parchment paper with water, open it, and place it directly over the stew. Cover the pot tightly with a lid and transfer to the oven. Cook for 1½ hours; check at least twice. The meat should be quite tender, but if you are going to freeze it, it must not be falling off the bone. If serving on the day of cooking, cook for an additional 30 minutes or until the rabbit is falling off the bone; the juices should be quite runny. Discard the bouquet of herbs. Add the vinegar, taste, and adjust the seasoning if necessary. Serve.

To freeze: Even if the stew was not cooked for that final 30 minutes, still add the vinegar and discard the herbs. Allow to cool completely to room temperature. Divide the stew among three 1-quart freezer bags, adding enough shallots and liquid to cover the meat. Seal, removing as much air as possible. Freeze flat until solid, about 2½ hours. Rearrange in the freezer once solid.

To thaw: Place the bags of stew on a plate. Thaw in the refrigerator overnight or until soft and ice free.

To serve: Preheat the oven to 375°F. Transfer the stew to an ovenproof dish. Dampen a piece of crumpled parchment paper with water, open it, and place directly over the stew. Cover the dish with a tight-fitting lid. Bake for 30 minutes or until the meat is completely heated through and falling from the bone. Serve immediately.

Sweet and crisp pies, crumbly strudels, light and airy phyllo packages—homemade pies and tarts are unbeatable and well worth the effort, with satisfying results every time. While they take some patience and a light hand to prepare, the best time to embark on such a project is not when friends and guests are due to arrive in an hour. This is where the freezer comes in handy, as most homemade pies and tarts freeze quite well. Keeping frozen tart shells or some pastry doughs on hand means that sweet and savory dishes can be put together in very little time. Also included in this chapter are an assortment of bake-ahead sweet and savory pies and tarts, ready to pop in the oven straight from the freezer.

pastry

Phyllo

For me, phyllo is one of the easiest and fastest pastries to use—no rolling, no dusting of flour and so on—but it's important to start with a good product! Most local Greek and Middle Eastern bakeries sell fresh, excellent-quality phyllo pastry. Frozen phyllo is good as well. The brands are endless, some a little thicker than others, which makes them slightly easier to work with (not necessarily authentic), but overall, pastry you'd rather buy than attempt to make at home.

If you intend to freeze any of the dishes using phyllo in this chapter, seek out fresh phyllo pastry, as this will freeze the best. Yes, you can refreeze phyllo, but do not refreeze the same pastry more than once, as the finished product will dry and flake too much on cooking.

When working with phyllo pastry:

❄ Keep it covered at all times when you are not working with it. I find the advice to use a damp kitchen towel unhelpful, as it spoils that top sheet of pastry every time, causing it to pucker and become sticky. I use a big sheet of plastic wrap lightly dusted with flour to stop it from sticking everywhere.

❄ Butter each layer of phyllo well, as this will allow the sheets to stay separate on baking. Make sure the butter is warm—it'll allow you to spread very thinly, as opposed to being thick if cool and starting to solidify.

❄ If the filling is very juicy, adding dried bread crumbs, cake crumbs, or nuts between every 2 to 3 layers is a good way of preventing soggy phyllo. This method is used for the Mixed Berry Phyllo Packages (page 161) and Apple Strudel (page 168).

❄ When rolling phyllo around the filling, you need to keep it loose; otherwise, when juices start to bubble during baking, the pastry will burst open.

❄ I find phyllo reheated the next day is very good, as it becomes even crispier than on the day of cooking. So don't be afraid of reheating leftover phyllo pie. Simply wrap well in foil, reheat for 5 to 8 minutes in a hot oven for the filling to heat through, then remove the foil and bake for another 5 minutes for the pastry to crisp up.

❄ Do not reheat phyllo, or any pastry pies for that matter, in the microwave oven. It'll be a disaster every time—one soggy mess!

Puff Pastry

Making puff pastry is time-consuming and somewhat difficult. A good selection of ready-made puff pastry is available in the freezer section of most supermarkets. My favorite brand in the United States is Dufour.

Here are some tips for using puff pastry:

* Thaw the pastry at room temperature for 30 minutes or until the block or roll is malleable; it should still feel cold. Or thaw in the refrigerator for 1 hour until malleable.

* Open or unroll the sheet of thawed puff pastry to lie flat on a lightly floured surface. Fold the pastry by bringing the left-hand end two-thirds of the way in, and the right-hand end in one-third of the way, finishing with an oblong of pastry about 4 inches wide and 8 inches long (different brands vary in size). With a rolling pin, roll out the dough about 1/4 inch thick. Repeat the folding and rolling twice more before rolling it to the size required. This ensures that the layers rise evenly during baking.

* When making a pie in a pie plate, the dish should have a lip around the perimeter—at least 1/4 to 3/4 inch. This allows the pastry to rest comfortably and prevents it from falling into the pie while baking.

* If you are not going to use a layer of pastry to line the sides and base of the pie dish, then to achieve a beautiful, even rise around the sides, put a strip of pastry on the rim first. Lay the rolled-out strips (the same width as dish rim) around the rim. Brush with water, then lay the top crust on it. Press to seal, then trim to neaten.

* Once the pie is assembled and sealed (whether in a pie dish or a flat pie), the ends of the cut pastry have been pushed together. Gently tap these ends with the blade of a sharp knife to separate the layers again, which will allow them to separate and rise evenly on baking.

* Make a hole or several decorative vents in the top of the pie to allow steam to escape during cooking.

* Chill the unbaked pie for at least 30 minutes before baking to allow the pastry to relax and prevent any dramatic shrinkage.

* Place a rack in the upper third of the oven. Preheat the oven to 425°F. Bake the puff pastry pie for 15 minutes at the high temperature so the pastry rises, then reduce the oven to 350°F for the rest of the recommended time.

Rich Pastry Dough

This is the classic pastry I use for pies and tarts. I prefer to use all butter in my pastry for its flavor and color, but if you like a flakier crust, then use equal amounts of butter and vegetable shortening. This dough is perfect for the Mediterranean Vegetable and Pine Nut Tart (page 144) or the Individual Zucchini and Robiola Cheese Tarts (page 147).

This recipe makes enough dough for a 9 to 10-inch tart pan; four 3-inch individual tart pans; one 10 × 15-inch baking sheet; or a 9 to 10-inch pie pan. The pastry can be frozen raw as a dough; unbaked, rolled in the tart pan; or baked blind, then frozen.

1⅓ cups all-purpose flour

⅛ teaspoon fine salt

8 tablespoons (1 stick) unsalted
  butter, chilled and diced

1 large egg, separated

1 to 2 tablespoons ice cold water

FREEZE FOR UP TO 4 WEEKS

1. Sift the flour and salt into a food processor. Add the butter and pulse for 1 to 2 minutes until the mixture resembles coarse meal. There should not be any large lumps of butter. Whisk the egg yolk with the water in a small bowl. Gradually add to the flour mixture and pulse until it clumps together. Transfer to a large bowl and bring the mixture together with your hands to form a dough.

2. Knead the dough for 1 minute on a clean surface until smooth. Flatten the dough into a disc about $^3/_4$ inch thick. Wrap in plastic wrap and refrigerate for at least 30 minutes, or freeze at this stage.

3. If the dough is too cold, allow it to warm up a bit; otherwise it will break on rolling out. Roll out on a clean surface, adding very little flour, if any. Thinly roll out to ⅛ inch. Lay half of the dough over the rolling pin and gently lift the rolling pin to transfer the pastry to the required tart pan. If using individual pans, divide or cut out the rolled pastry using a pastry cutter before lifting and pressing into the pans. Gently ease into all corners of the pan, pressing into the fluted edge with your index finger. Prick the base with a fork. Freeze for 20 minutes before baking blind or freeze until solid if to be stored unbaked.

> *continued*

4. To bake blind, preheat the oven to 400°F. Place a rack in the top third of the oven. Preheat a baking sheet in the oven. Crumple a piece of parchment paper large enough to line the base and sides of the tart pan. Open it and place it directly on the chilled pastry. Fill with baking beans or pie weights. Place the chilled tart on the preheated baking sheet and bake for 15 minutes; the pastry should be completely set and just tinged with color. Remove the paper, lifting out the beans at the same time. Return the tart to the oven for another 4 to 5 minutes until golden brown. Beat the egg white with about 1 tablespoon water and brush the inside of the tart; this will seal the pastry. Return to the oven and bake for another 2 minutes. Remove and place on a wire rack. Leave until cooled to room temperature.

To freeze: To freeze the pastry dough, don't roll it out. Wrap in plastic freezer wrap, then heavy-duty foil. Freeze until required.

To freeze the unbaked pastry shell, place the pastry-lined tart pan on a baking sheet and freeze until solid, about 1½ hours. If freezing for 2 to 3 weeks, gently ease out of the pan, cover with plastic freezer wrap, and store in an airtight plastic container to protect from heavier objects in the freezer.

To freeze a baked pastry shell, remove from the tart pan once cooled completely. Place on a baking sheet and freeze until solid, about 1½ hours. Cover with plastic freezer wrap, place in a plastic container, and store in the freezer.

To thaw: The raw pastry dough needs to thaw. Remove the foil and plastic wrap. Place on a paper-towel-lined plate; cover loosely with plastic wrap, and thaw in the refrigerator for 4 hours or overnight, until completely soft.

To cook: The uncooked pastry shells can be cooked from frozen. Remove from the freezer, discard the wrapping, and gently ease back in their tart pan(s). Continue as instructed by the recipe.

Sweet Rich Pastry Dough

Use this pastry for sweet pies and tarts such as the Peaches and Cream Pie (page 163) or the Blueberry and Pear Pie (page 166).

This dough is sufficient for one 9 to 10-inch tart pan, four 3-inch individual tart pans, or a double crust for a 9 to 10-inch pie. Store, bake, and freeze as for Rich Pastry Dough.

1⅓ cups all-purpose flour

Pinch of fine salt

2 tablespoons confectioners' sugar

8 tablespoons (1 stick) unsalted
 butter, chilled and diced

1 large egg, separated

2 tablespoons ice cold water

FREEZE FOR UP TO 4 WEEKS

1. Sift the flour, salt, and sugar into a food processor. Add the butter and pulse for 1 to 2 minutes until the mixture resembles coarse meal. There should not be any large lumps of butter. Whisk the egg yolk with the water in a small bowl. Gradually add to the flour mixture and pulse until it clumps together.

2. Transfer to a large bowl and bring the mixture together with your hands to form a dough. Knead the dough for 1 minute on a clean surface until smooth. Flatten the dough into a disc about ³/₄ inch thick. Wrap in plastic wrap and refrigerate for at least 30 minutes, or freeze at this stage. Continue as per the method for Rich Pastry Dough.

Choux Pastry

This pastry is more of a batter or paste than a dough. The baked choux buns can be frozen with or without fillings. The choux buns can be used for savory or sweet fillings such as Chocolate Profiteroles (page 170). For savory fillings, mix small cooked shrimp with mayonnaise and chives; or mix cream cheese with chopped red onions and smoked salmon. Or fill with smooth chicken liver paté and chopped cornichons.

2 cups hot water

1 cup all-purpose flour

½ teaspoon fine salt

6 tablespoons unsalted butter, cut
   into 6 pieces

4 large eggs, lightly beaten

MAKES 32 TO 34 BUNS

FREEZE FOR UP TO 2 WEEKS

1. Preheat the oven to 425°F. Place a rack in the top third of the oven. Place the water in a small ovenproof bowl and set on the floor of the oven (this will create steam in the oven and help the pastry to puff). Lightly grease two heavy baking sheets, then dust with flour. Set aside.

2. To prepare the paste, sift the flour and salt onto a piece of parchment paper. Set aside. Place 1 cup water and the butter in a small pot and heat over low heat until the butter melts. Increase the heat and bring the mixture to a boil. Leaving the heat on high, remove from the stove. Immediately add the flour to the water mixture and beat with a wooden spoon until a stiff paste forms. Return to the stove and beat over high heat for 2 minutes or until the mixture comes clean away from the sides of the pot and looks smooth, thick, and glossy.

3. Transfer the batter to a standing mixer and beat with the paddle attachment to cool slightly. While the mixer is running, gradually add the eggs, about 3 tablespoons eggs at a time, beating well between each addition. The process should take 3 to 5 minutes; the mixture will be smooth and shiny and should hold stiff peaks.

4. Using 2 teaspoons, scoop and scrape up heaping spoonfuls of pastry batter and lay on the prepared baking sheets; space well apart, about 2 inches. Allow 16 to 17 choux buns for each baking sheet.

5. Bake for 20 minutes or until the pastry has puffed and is golden brown. Remove from the oven and, using a sharp paring knife, pierce a hole in the side of each bun. Return the buns to the oven and bake for 3 to 5 minutes to allow the interior steam to escape and dry out. Remove from the oven and allow to cool completely on a wire rack.

To freeze: Once the choux buns are cooled, place them on a baking sheet, leaving about 1 inch between them. Open freeze until solid, about 1 hour. Place in an airtight container and freeze until required.

To thaw: Preheat the oven to 400°F. Place the frozen choux buns on a baking sheet and reheat for 5 minutes or until thawed and crisp. Let cool completely before filling and serving.

Mixed Greens and Feta Pie

Make the most of early summer greens such as dandelion leaves, spinach, arugula, watercress, beet leaves, and young chard leaves. Use any combination available or, if you prefer, you can just use spinach, as is traditionally used for spanakopita. If you like, cook the mixed greens ahead and keep them refrigerated for up to three days. Serve this flaky vegetable pie as an appetizer or as a main course with a bean salad or cucumber and tomato salad.

2 pounds summer greens such as spinach, Swiss chard, watercress, arugula, or dandelion leaves, washed, trimmed, and chopped separately (any Swiss chard stems reserved)

Salt and freshly ground black pepper

2 tablespoons extra virgin olive oil

1 onion, chopped

2 garlic cloves, finely chopped

2 tablespoons chopped fresh tarragon or oregano

Eight 12 × 16-inch phyllo pastry sheets, thawed if frozen

4 tablespoons (½ stick) unsalted butter, melted

5 ounces fresh Greek feta, crumbled into large lumps

SERVES 8

FREEZE FOR UP TO 2 WEEKS

1. Place the tougher greens such as Swiss chard and dandelion leaves in a large pot. Cover and cook over low heat for 5 minutes, stirring occasionally, until the greens start to wilt; add the more delicate greens such as watercress and argula. Season with salt and pepper to taste. Cook for 3 to 5 minutes more; once the greens are wilted, transfer them to a sieve placed over a bowl. Allow the juices to drain, gently pushing down on the greens to extract as much excess liquid as possible. Discard the liquid and set the greens aside to cool.

2. Meanwhile, heat the oil in a skillet over medium heat. Add the onion and cook for 5 to 8 minutes until soft. Add the garlic and cook for 1 minute. Add the chopped Swiss chard stems, if using, and cook for another 5 minutes. Add the tarragon and cook for 1 minute. Remove from the heat. Mix together the onion and cooked greens in a bowl. Taste and adjust the seasoning. Let stand until cool. The mixture can be refrigerated at this stage for up to 3 days.

3. Preheat the oven to 375°F. Place a rack in the upper third of the oven.

> *continued*

4. Open the phyllo pastry on a clean surface and cut the pastry in half to form 6 × 8-inch rectangles. Gather the rectangles up into one pile. Keep the top of the pastry covered with plastic wrap while not using. Place one sheet of pastry on a clean surface. Brush with butter. Lift the pastry and use it to line a 9 to 10-inch tart pan (about 1 inch deep). Continue to butter and layer ten sheets of the pastry, overlapping them along the bottom and sides of the tart pan and allowing the pastry edges to hang over the sides of the pan.

5. Spread half of the greens mixture in the the pastry shell. Sprinkle with feta, then top with another layer of the greens. Brush another three sheets of the pastry and lay them over the filling to cover completely. Fold in the edges of the overhanging pastry sheets. Butter the remaining pastry sheets and roughly place on the top of the pie, allowing it to look ruffled. Brush with the remaining butter.

6. Bake the pie for 1 hour and 15 minutes, covering halfway through with foil, until the pastry is crisp and golden brown. Serve warm or at room temperature.

To freeze: Freeze the pie prior to baking. Freeze in the tart pan until solid, about 2 hours. Lift the tart out of the pan, and cover with plastic freezer wrap, then heavy-duty foil. Freeze until required.

To thaw: Remove the tart from the freezer, uncover, and return to the tart pan. Place in the refrigerator and partially thaw for 4 hours or overnight.

To cook: Preheat the oven to 350°F; place a rack in the center of the oven. Bake for 1 hour and 30 minutes, or until golden brown and the filling is heated through, covering with foil three-quarters of the way through. Serve warm or at room temperature.

Mediterranean Vegetable and Pine Nut Tart

This tart is excellent served warm or cold with a creamy goat cheese as an appetizer or light lunch. It also makes a nice accompaniment to grilled lamb chops, steak, or chicken.

Choose small to medium-size seasonal vegetables; the larger ones tend to be watery and will cause a soggy pastry if your intention is to freeze the tart.

One 9 to 10-inch frozen unbaked, Rich Pastry shell (page 134)

1 egg white beaten with 1 tablespoon water

2 pounds mixed Mediterranean vegetables such as bell peppers, zucchini, summer squash, red onions, and eggplants

3 tablespoons extra virgin olive oil

1 tablespoon balsamic vinegar

Sea salt flakes and freshly ground black pepper

2 tablespoons pine nuts, toasted

Arugula tossed with extra vinegar and olive oil for serving

SERVES 6 TO 8

FREEZE FOR UP TO 4 WEEKS

1. Preheat the oven to 400°F. Place a rack in the top third of the oven. Add a baking sheet to preheat.

2. Return the frozen pastry shell to the tart pan. Line the pastry with parchment paper and fill with pie weights. Bake for 15 minutes or until just golden and set. Remove the parchment and pie weights. Return to the oven and bake for 4 to 5 minutes to dry out. Brush the bottom and sides of the tart shell with the egg white. Bake for another 3 to 5 minutes until golden brown and cooked through. Let cool on a rack for 10 minutes. Remove the tart shell from the tart pan and place on the rack.

3. If using peppers, rub them with a little oil, place on a baking pan, and roast for 25 minutes in the oven at 400°F, turning frequently until charred. Transfer to a bowl, cover with plastic wrap, and let cool. Once cool, remove the core, skin, and seeds from the peppers and cut into quarters. Set aside. Meanwhile, wash and trim the zucchini, squash, and eggplants. Pat dry with paper towels. Cut the vegetables lengthwise, about ⅓ inch thick. Slice the onions into ¼-inch-thick rings.

4. Over high heat, preheat a grill pan until very hot. Brush with 1 to 2 teaspoons of the oil. Add the vegetables and grill for 3 minutes on each side. Meanwhile, whisk together the remaining oil and the vinegar in a large bowl. Transfer the grilled vegetables to the bowl with the dressing. Add the peppers, if using, and toss to mix with dressing. Taste and season with salt and pepper to taste. Allow to stand for 10 minutes.

5. To serve without freezing, assemble the grilled vegetable salad in the warm crust. Sprinkle with pine nuts. Cut into wedges and serve each wedge topped with arugula and a drizzle of vinegar and olive oil.

To freeze: Leave the baked crust in the tart pan until cooled to room temperature. Assemble the cooled grilled vegetables in the tart shell. Sprinkle with pine nuts and about 1 tablespoon of the remaining dressing in the bowl. Freeze in the tart pan until solid, about 1½ hours. Carefully remove the tart from the tart pan. Wrap the tart first in plastic freezer wrap, then in heavy-duty foil. Freeze until required.

To thaw: Remove the wrapping from the frozen tart and return to the tart pan. Cover loosely with plastic wrap and thaw overnight in the fridge.

To serve: Preheat the oven to 400°F. Place a rack in the center of the oven. To reheat the thawed tart, place on a baking sheet and bake for 30 minutes. To serve straight from the freezer, remove the foil and plastic wrap from the tart. Return the tart to the tart pan. Place on a baking sheet and bake for 1 hour or until heated through, covering with foil halfway through.

Individual Zucchini and Robiola Cheese Tarts

Serve these tarts as an appetizer or lunch, accompanied by a salad of bitter and peppery greens (such as watercress, arugula, dandelion, radicchio, Belgian endive, or frisée) to complement the rich, creamy texture of the tarts.

Robiola is an Italian cheese usually produced from cow's milk, but some versions are made solely with goat's milk or a mixture of cow's milk and sheep's or goat's milk.

Eight 3-inch frozen uncooked
Rich Pastry shells (page 134)

1 egg white beaten with
1 tablespoon water

¼ cup extra virgin olive oil

1½ pounds zucchini (about 4 in
total), cut into ¼-inch rounds

2 small onions, finely chopped

2 garlic cloves, crushed to a paste
with ½ teaspoon sea salt flakes

1 tablespoon chopped fresh
tarragon

Salt and freshly ground black
pepper

4 ounces aged Robiola, cut into
small cubes

½ cup half-and-half

½ cup heavy cream

2 large eggs

MAKES 8 TARTS

FREEZE FOR UP TO 2 WEEKS

1. Preheat the oven to 400°F. Place racks in the top and middle of the oven.

2. Put the frozen pastry shells back in the tart pans. Line the tart shells with parchment paper and fill with pie weights. Bake the tart shells for 15 minutes. The shells in the middle of the oven will need an extra 5 minutes. Reduce the oven temperature to 350°F. Remove the parchment and pie weights. Brush the inside of the tart shells with egg white to seal the pastry. Bake for another 5 to 8 minutes until golden brown.

3. Heat 2 tablespoons of the oil in a large skillet over medium heat. Add half of the zucchini and sauté until golden brown on both sides, about 5 minutes. Transfer to a plate lined with paper towels. Repeat with the remaining oil and zucchini. Add the onions and garlic to the skillet and cook for 3 to 5 minutes until the onions are soft. Return the zucchini to the pan. Add the tarragon and season with salt and pepper to taste. Set aside to cool.

> *continued*

4. Divide the cooled zucchini mixture and cheese among the tart shells. Beat together the half-and-half, cream, and eggs in a bowl. Divide the mixture equally among the tart shells, filling to about ¼ inch below the rim. Bake for 20 minutes or until golden brown and the filling is just slightly set. Allow the tarts to cool for 10 minutes before serving.

To freeze: Do not bake the filled tarts. Once cooled to room temperature, place on a baking sheet and freeze until solid, about 1 hour. Once solid, lift the tarts out of the pans and transfer to a plastic container, separating with waxed paper. Return to the freezer.

To cook: Preheat the oven to 375°F. Place a rack in the center and middle of the oven. Return the tarts to the tart pans, place on the baking sheets, and cover with foil. Bake for 30 minutes, uncover, and cook for another 15 minutes or until golden brown and just set. Allow the tarts to stand for 10 minutes before serving.

Pissaladière

Serve as a snack or as an accompaniment to grilled or baked sausages (spicy or turkey) with Dijon mustard. Together they make an excellent brunch main course. Or to serve as an hors d'oeuvre, cut the pastry into small triangles before adding the caramelized onions.

2 tablespoons extra virgin olive oil,
    plus extra for drizzling

2 tablespoons unsalted butter

3 pounds sweet onions, cut into
    $1/3$-inch-thick wedges

1 tablespoon fresh thyme leaves

1 tablespoon honey

2 tablespoons chopped fresh
    flat-leaf parsley

Salt and black pepper

Rich Pastry Dough (page 134)
    made with 2 tablespoons finely
    grated Parmesan, thawed if frozen

1 egg white beaten with 1
    tablespoon water

2 tablespoons Dijon mustard

One 3-ounce jar anchovy fillets in
    oil, drained

3 ounces (heaping $1/4$ cup) black
    olives, halved and pitted

**SERVES 12 AS AN HORS D'OEUVRE,
OR 8 AS A SIDE DISH
FREEZE FOR UP TO 3 WEEKS**

1. Heat the 2 tablespoons oil in a large skillet over medium heat. Add the butter and when foaming, add the onions, thyme, and honey. Stir to mix (if the pan is not quite large enough, start with some of the onions, then add the others as the first batch begins to reduce, about 5 minutes). Reduce the heat to low, cover the pan, and cook the onions for 20 minutes. Uncover, increase the heat, and cook for another 20 minutes or until the onions are a golden caramel color and all of the liquid has evaporated. Stir in the parsley and season with salt and pepper to taste. Set the onions aside and allow to cool.

2. Preheat the oven to 400°F. Place a rack in the top third of the oven.

3. Thinly roll out the pastry onto a lightly floured surface, large enough to line a shallow 10 × 15-inch baking pan. Lift the pastry onto the baking pan and trim the edges to neaten and prick all over with a fork. Refrigerate or freeze for 30 minutes.

> *continued*

4. Remove the pastry from the refrigerator, line with parchment paper, and fill with pie weights. Bake for 10 to 15 minutes until the crust is set and just beginning to brown. Remove the pie weights and parchment. Brush the crust with the beaten egg white to seal the pastry. Return to the oven and bake for 5 to 8 minutes until golden brown.

5. Reduce the oven temperature to 350°F. Spread the mustard along the bottom of the crust and top with the caramelized onions while the crust is still warm. Arrange the anchovies in a lattice pattern on top of the onions. Dot with the olives. Drizzle with a little olive oil and bake for 20 to 25 minutes until heated through and sizzling. Serve warm or at room temperature.

To freeze: Spread the mustard along the bottom of the baked crust. Cut the pastry into 3 × 2-inch rectangles and let cool completely to room temperature. Line a baking sheet with parchment paper. Lift the individual pastry rectangles with a metal spatula onto the prepared baking sheet, leaving about 1 inch between them. Divide the onion mixture among the pastry triangles, going as close to the edge as possible. Top with one or two anchovy fillets, then dot with the olives. Freeze until solid, about 1 hour. Transfer to a freezer-safe plastic container, separating the pastries with waxed paper. Cover and freeze.

To cook: Cook straight from the freezer. Preheat the oven to 400°F. Place a rack in the center of the oven. Place the pissaladière triangles on a baking sheet lined with parchment paper. Cover with foil and bake for 20 minutes. Remove the foil and bake for another 10 minutes or until golden brown. Serve warm.

Smoked Paprika Steak Pie

This pie is the perfect recipe to use up leftover steak. You can use a variety of good cuts, including sirloin, porterhouse, and rib-eye.

FILLING

1 pound waxy potatoes, such as
   Yukon Gold

1½ pounds sirloin steak, about 1
   inch thick

3 tablespoons olive oil

Salt and freshly ground black
   pepper

2 tablespoons unsalted butter

2 onions, halved and thinly sliced

1 tablespoon smoked paprika
   (dulce)

1½ teaspoons crushed red pepper

½ teaspoon ground cumin

½ cup ready-made beef demi-
   glace or thin gravy

1 cup beef stock

2 ounces (¼ cup) kalamata olives,
   pitted and halved

SERVES 4 TO 6

FREEZE FOR UP TO 3 WEEKS

1. Pierce the potatoes a few times with a fork. Place in a large pot and cover with water. Bring to a boil and cook for 20 minutes or until just tender but not cooked all the way through. Drain and let cool.

2. Cut the steak into three equal portions. Rub with 1 teaspoon of the oil and season with salt and pepper.

3. Heat a skillet over medium-high heat until hot. Sear the steak for 4 minutes on each side. Set aside and let stand for 10 minutes.

4. Heat the remaining oil in the skillet over medium heat. Add the butter and when foaming, add the onions and cook for 5 to 8 minutes until soft. Add the smoked paprika, red pepper, and cumin and cook for 3 minutes. Add the beef demi-glace and stock and bring to a boil.

5. Meanwhile, peel the cooled potatoes and cut into discs about ⅓ inch thick. Cut the seared beef into ¼-inch-thick slices, cutting against the grain. Add the potatoes, steak, and olives to the onion mixture. Taste and adjust the seasoning. Remove from the heat and let cool.

6. Preheat the oven to 375°F. Place a rack in the center of the oven.

> *continued*

3½ cups plus 1½ tablespoons
   all-purpose flour

¾ cup solid vegetable shortening

½ cup milk

1 teaspoon fine salt

1 egg yolk beaten with 1 tablespoon milk

7. To make the pastry, sift the flour into a large bowl and make a well in the center. Bring the vegetable shortening, milk, salt, and ½ cup water to a boil in a small pot, allowing the shortening to fully melt. Pour the mixture into the flour and mix with a large wooden spoon to combine. Allow the mixture to cool slightly until you can touch the dough. Turn out onto a floured surface and knead until smooth. The pastry will firm up upon cooling; do not be tempted to add extra flour. If too wet, chill to firm up faster.

8. Transfer the filling into a 9 × 13-inch dish. Roll out the pastry on a lightly floured surface to form a 11 × 14-inch rectangle. Trim the edges to neaten. Lay half of the pastry over a rolling pin and gently lift the rolling pin to transfer the dough to fit over the filling, allowing the pastry to drape over the sides of the dish. Make a small hole at the top to allow steam to escape while cooking. Brush the top with the egg glaze. Bake for 50 minutes or until the pastry is golden brown and crisp. Allow the pie to stand for 10 minutes before serving.

To freeze: Allow the filling to cool completely to room temperature before topping with the pastry. Do not glaze the pastry. Freeze, uncovered, until solid, about 2 hours. Cover the top of the pie with plastic freezer wrap, then heavy-duty foil. Freeze.

To thaw: Remove the pie the day before required and remove the foil and plastic covering. Let thaw in the fridge overnight.

To cook: Preheat the oven to 400°F. Place a rack in the center of the oven. Allow the pie to stand at room temperature for 15 minutes, then glaze with the egg mixture. Place on a baking sheet and bake for 35 to 40 minutes until the pastry is golden and the filling is heated through. Allow the pie to stand for 10 minutes before serving.

Individual Chicken and Leek Pot Pies

Step one is also how I choose to make fresh chicken stock. Remember not to cook the chicken stock too quickly—always keep the heat medium to low for a gentle simmer, or the stock will turn out cloudy.

If you are not planning to use the chicken for the pie, simply use it for chicken salad. For the salad, remove the meat from the carcass and mix with mayonnaise, crème fraîche, chopped cornichons, and chopped fresh flat-leaf parsley. Season to taste.

One 4-pound organic chicken, washed and patted dry

1 onion, quartered

6 large carrots, peeled, 1 quartered, 5 cut into 1-inch pieces

4 large fresh flat-leaf parsley sprigs

6 tablespoons butter

6 leeks, white and light green parts only, washed and cut into 2-inch pieces

2 tablespoons fresh thyme leaves

3 tablespoons all-purpose flour, plus some for rolling

1 cup milk

Salt and freshly ground black pepper

1½ pounds puff pastry, thawed if frozen (see page 133 for tips)

1 egg yolk beaten with 1 tablespoon milk

SERVES 6

FREEZE FOR UP TO 4 WEEKS

1. Place the chicken in a large deep pot along with the onion, quartered carrot, and parsley sprigs. Add enough cold water to cover. Bring to a boil, skimming the surface of any scum that appears. Reduce the heat to a simmer and cook until the chicken is cooked through, about 45 minutes. Remove the chicken and let cool. Allow the stock to cool as well. Line a sieve with a paper towels and gradually ladle the stock through to strain, discarding the onion carrot, and parsley. Reserve 1½ cups stock. Cool the remaining stock and package in 1-quart bags and freeze for another use.

2. To prepare the leeks, melt 2 tablespoons of the butter in a pot over low heat. When foaming add the leeks. Dampen a large piece of crumpled parchment paper with water, open it, and place directly over the leeks. Cover and cook slowly for 10 minutes. The leeks should sweat and not take on any color. Add the remaining carrots to the leeks and cover once more.

> *continued*

Cook for another 10 minutes. Once again, the vegetables should not brown. Remove the lid and paper and cook for another 5 minutes or until all of the liquid evaporates. Transfer the vegetables into a large bowl and set aside. Reserve the pot for later use.

3. Remove the chicken from the carcass, picking all the meat from the bones. Discard the skin and bones. Shred the chicken meat into large pieces. Add to the vegetables. Stir in the thyme leaves.

4. Melt the remaining butter in the pot the vegetables were cooked in. Add the 3 tablespoons flour and cook for 2 minutes, stirring to make a roux. Remove the pot from the heat and gradually stir in the reserved stock, followed by the milk. Return to the heat and cook, stirring constantly, for 5 to 8 minutes until the sauce is bubbling and thick; it should thickly coat the back of a wooden spoon. Add the sauce to the chicken mixture and season with salt and pepper to taste. Spoon the pie filling into six 1-cup oval pie dishes or individual pie plates.

5. Fold and roll the pastry, following the instructions on page 135. Divide the pastry into thirds and roll out each to about ¼ inch thick. Cut ¼- to ½-inch-wide strips from each side of the pastry and dampen with water, then secure around the rim of each pie plate. Halve each piece of the pastry (each should be large enough to cover a pie plate). First, wet the prepared pastry rim, then drape the large piece of pastry over the pie, easing out the air between the filling and pastry as you smooth the pastry over the filling. Press the edges together, then trim with a small sharp knife. Press the edges again to seal. Tap the cut edges with the blade of a sharp knife to separate the layers. Make a hole in the center of each pie to allow the steam to escape during cooking. Refrigerate the pies for 20 minutes.

6. Preheat the oven to 425°F. Place a rack in the center of the oven.

7. Place the pies on a large baking sheet, about three to each sheet, and brush the tops with the egg glaze. Bake for 15 to 20 minutes until golden. Reduce the oven temperature to 350°F and bake for another 20 minutes, covering the pies loosely with foil if they are browning too quickly. Allow the pies to stand for 5 minutes before serving.

To freeze: Freeze the pies before they are baked. The filling must be completely cooled to room temperature before the pastry is placed on top. Do not glaze. Freeze the pies, uncovered, until solid, about 1$\frac{1}{2}$ hours. Cover with plastic freezer wrap followed by heavy-duty foil.

To thaw: Remove the foil and plastic wrap from each pie and thaw the pies overnight in the refrigerator.

To cook: Preheat the oven to 425°F. Place a rack in the center of the oven. Glaze the pies with the egg yolk mixture. Place three pies on each baking sheet and bake for 20 minutes. Reduce the oven temperature to 350°F and bake for another 15 minutes or until the pastry is golden and the filling is bubbling through the edges of the crust. Cover with foil if the pastry is browning too quickly. Allow the pies to stand for 5 minutes before serving.

Shrimp Spring Rolls with Thai Dipping Sauce

These excellent rolls can be served as an appetizer or as hors d'oeuvres to accompany cocktails. Make the dipping sauce on the day required.

FILLING

12 large shrimp, peeled, deveined,
    and coarsely chopped

1½ teaspoons sambal oelek (chile
    garlic sauce)

1 tablespoon fish sauce

1 tablespoon soy sauce

1 tablespoon cornstarch

1 large carrot, peeled and cut into
    thin 1-inch-long sticks

4 scallions, white and light green
    parts only, thinly sliced into
    1-inch-long strips

2 ounces bean sprouts

Seven 12 × 16-inch sheets phyllo
    pastry, thawed if frozen
    (see page 132 for tips)

4 tablespoons (½ stick) unsalted
    butter, melted

MAKES 28 ROLLS

FREEZE FOR UP TO 3 WEEKS

1. Place the shrimp and sambal oelek in a large bowl. Combine the fish sauce and soy sauce in a small bowl, then stir in the cornstarch until smooth. Add to the shrimp. Add the carrot, scallions, and bean sprouts and toss to coat.

2. Unroll the phyllo pastry and place on a large cutting board. First, cut in half to produce fourteen 12 × 8-inch rectangles, then cut once more to make twenty-eight 6 × 4-inch rectangles. Gather the pastry rectangles together in one pile and drape with plastic wrap to prevent them from drying out.

3. Place one sheet of phyllo on a clean surface, with the shorter end facing you. Brush with melted butter and put 1 tablespoon of filling at the end closest to you. Roll the phyllo around the filling. Once rolled halfway, fold in the two ends to completely enclose the filling. Continue to roll. Coat with more butter and place the filled pastry on a large baking sheet lined with parchment paper. Continue until you've made 28 rolls. Refrigerate for 20 minutes.

2 garlic cloves, finely chopped

2-inch piece fresh ginger, peeled
   and finely chopped

1 small Thai green chile, finely
   chopped

2 teaspoons sugar

2 tablespoons fresh lime juice

2 tablespoons fish sauce

1 tablespoon rice vinegar

4. Preheat the oven to $375°$F. Place a rack in the center of the oven.

5. Bake the spring rolls for 20 to 25 minutes until golden brown and crisp all the way through. Cool for 10 minutes before serving.

6. Meanwhile, make the dipping sauce by combining all the ingredients together in a bowl. Serve alongside the warm spring rolls.

To freeze: Do not bake the assembled spring rolls. Place the rolls on a large baking sheet lined with plastic wrap, allowing about 1 inch between them. Open freeze until solid, about 1 hour. Once the spring rolls are frozen solid, pack them into a freezer-safe plastic container, separating the layers of spring rolls with plastic freezer wrap or freezer paper.

To cook: Preheat the oven to 375°F. Place a rack in the center of the oven. Place the spring rolls on a baking sheet, brush with oil, and bake straight from the freezer for 30 to 40 minutes until golden brown and the filling is heated through. Allow the spring rolls to cool slightly before serving. Make the dipping sauce on the day of serving.

Ice Cream and Mixed Berry Phyllo Packages

This new twist on Baked Alaska features an assortment of berries and ice cream wrapped in a purse-style package of layered phyllo pastry. The parcels are baked straight from the freezer, allowing the ice cream inside to partially melt and combine with the juice from the berries. The pastry, however, remains crisp. The goal when making these is to keep the pastry light, using as little as possible to avoid a doughy center in the twisty part of the parcel. Use your favorite flavor of homemade or store-bought hard-packed ice cream (the soft scoop variety will melt too quickly when baked).

1 pint ice cream

8 tablespoons (1 stick) unsalted butter

¼ cup fresh fine bread crumbs

2 tablespoons coarsely ground almonds

1 cup blueberries

1 cup raspberries

1 cup strawberries

Sixteen 12 × 16-inch sheets of frozen phyllo pastry (see page 132 for tips)

2 tablespoons confectioners' sugar, plus more for dusting

MAKES 8 PACKAGES

FREEZE FOR UP TO 1 WEEK

1. Place a baking sheet lined with plastic wrap in the freezer to chill. Remove the ice cream from the freezer and allow to stand at room temperature until scoopable. Scoop eight balls of ice cream and place on the baking sheet in the freezer. Freeze until solid, about 30 minutes.

2. Meanwhile, melt 2 tablespoons of the butter in a skillet over low heat. When foaming, add the bread crumbs and cook for 8 to 10 minutes until just golden, stirring frequently. Add the almonds and cook for another 1 to 2 minutes until they turn golden as well, stirring frequently to break up any large clumps of bread crumbs. Transfer to a paper-towel-lined plate and allow to cool.

3. Wash the berries and drain on paper towels. Hull the strawberries and halve or quarter them if large. Combine the berries in a bowl.

> *continued*

4. Unroll the sheets of phyllo pastry and place on a large cutting board. Cut in quarters to make 6 × 8-inch rectangles. Gather the rectangles into a pile. Set aside and drape with plastic wrap to prevent the pastry from drying out. You will need to work quickly when assembling the packages, so make sure all of the remaining ingredients are at the ready, including the confectioners' sugar (placed in a small fine sieve), the remaining butter (melted, with a pastry brush alongside), the cooled bread crumb and almond mixture, and the berries. The ice cream, however, should remain in the freezer, to be removed one scoop at a time as you work.

5. Place one sheet of phyllo vertically in front of you. Dust with confectioners' sugar. Place another sheet of pastry on top, horizontally. The two sheets should cross over in the middle. Brush them with butter. Sprinkle 1 to 2 tablespoons of the bread crumb mixture over the overlapping section. Add another piece of phyllo on top, on a diagonal (the left hand at 11 o'clock and the right hand at 5 o'clock). Brush with butter. Add a fourth layer of phyllo on the opposite diagonal angle. Brush with butter and sprinkle the center with another 1 to 2 tablespoons bread crumbs. Add a single layer of berries in the center. Top with a scoop of frozen ice cream. Working very quickly and gently, gather the pastry up around the ice cream and fruit, bringing the ends together, and twist gently just above the ice cream, allowing for some ends to stick up and others to drape over the twist. Brush all over with a little more butter. Place in the freezer on the chilled baking sheet. Freeze until solid, about 1 hour.

6. Preheat the oven to 375°F. Place a rack in the center of the oven. Place a baking sheet in the oven to preheat as well.

7. Transfer the packages to the preheated baking sheet and bake for 12 to 15 minutes, until the pastry is crisp and golden brown all over, including the bottom. Remove from the oven and place on serving plates. Dust with the remaining confectioners' sugar and serve immediately.

To freeze: Once the packages are frozen solid in the freezer, transfer them to a large, deep plastic container. If the container is tall enough, cover with a lid. Alternatively, place a large sheet of heavy-duty foil over the container.

To cook: Follow the instructions above, cooking the packages straight from the freezer.

Peaches and Cream Pie

The secret to preventing the peaches from getting mushy when baked is to work with large peach slices. The result is a luscious bite of peach that the crème fraîche has melted into.

The streusel or crumble topping, with its buttery-sweet taste and crisp to crunchy texture, is a good staple to have in the freezer; it can be simply scattered over soft fruit or apples and baked for a fruit cobbler. Or use it to top sweet muffins or cupcakes. Add sliced almonds, pecans, or hazelnuts as well. Bake straight from the freezer.

Sweet Rich Pastry Dough

    (page 137), thawed if frozen

TOPPING

¼ cup confectioners' sugar

¼ cup all-purpose flour

¼ teaspoon baking powder

Pinch of fine salt

4 tablespoons (½ stick) unsalted

    butter, diced and chilled

FILLING

1 egg white beaten with 1

    tablespoon water

5 to 6 (1½ pounds) ripe peaches

1 tablespoon lemon juice

¼ cup crème fraîche

SERVES 8

FREEZE FOR UP TO 1 MONTH

1. Thinly roll out the pastry to line a 9-inch metal pie plate, sprinkling lightly with flour if necessary. Place the pastry in the pie plate and trim the edges to allow a 1-inch overhang. Tuck the edge of the overhang under the lip of the pie. Scallop the edge with your index finger of one hand pushing into your thumb and index finger of the other hand. Pierce the base of the pastry with a fork. Freeze for 30 minutes.

2. Preheat the oven to 400°F. Place a rack in the top third of the oven; place a baking sheet in the oven to preheat at the same time.

3. To prepare the streusel topping, sift the confectioners' sugar with the flour, baking powder, and salt into a bowl. Add the butter and gently rub into the dry ingredients with your fingers, stopping once the mixture forms a coarse meal. You can also do this in a food processor. Refrigerate until required.

> *continued*

PEACH PIE 7/14/05

4. Line the pie plate with parchment paper and baking beans. Bake blind for 15 minutes. Remove the paper and baking beans and brush with the egg white to seal. Bake for another 5 minutes to dry the pastry a little more. Allow the pastry to cool slightly.

5. Reduce the oven temperature to 350°F. Cut the peaches into quarters, discarding the pits, and coat the peaches with lemon juice.

6. Spread 1 tablespoon crème fraîche in the base of the pie, then sprinkle one-third of the streusel mixture over the crème fraîche. Arrange the peaches skin side down in the pie and dot with the crème fraîche. Sprinkle over the remaining streusel topping.

7. Bake the pie for 40 minutes or until the cream is bubbling, the peaches are tender, and the streusel is golden brown. Allow the pie to cool for 15 minutes before serving.

To freeze: Allow the baked pie crust to cool completely to room temperature. Assemble as above and place in the freezer until solid, about 2 hours. If you are planning to freeze the pie for longer than one week, then remove from the pie plate once solid. Cover with plastic freezer wrap followed by heavy-duty foil. Freeze.

To bake: Bake the pie straight from the freezer. Preheat the oven to 375°F. Place a rack in the center of the oven. Place a baking sheet in the oven to preheat at the same time. Remove the foil and plastic wrap from the pie and return to the pie plate if necessary. Place the pie on the preheated baking sheet and cover loosely with foil. Bake for 35 minutes. Uncover the pie and cook for 1 hour or until golden brown and bubbling. Allow the pie to cool for 15 minutes before serving.

Blueberry and Pear Pie

If you intend to freeze the pie, first be sure to use an unfrozen pastry dough. Then I strongly recommend that you first open freeze the blueberries. This way they will not clump into one solid mass on freezing and will bake directly from the freezer far more evenly and quickly. (To open freeze the blueberries, simply spread the fruit on one or two baking sheets and freeze for one hour and thirty minutes or until solid.) If you make the topping in a lattice pattern, this will also mean a more even cooking for the filling.

Sweet Rich Pastry Dough

   (page 137)

2 tablespoons all-purpose flour

2 tablespoons cornstarch

¼ cup sugar, plus some for

   sprinkling

½ teaspoon ground cinnamon

2 tablespoons crème fraîche

3 pints (6 cups) blueberries

1 ripe pear, peeled, cored, and

   diced

1 egg yolk beaten with 2

   tablespoons milk

SERVES 8

FREEZE FOR UP TO 1 MONTH

1. On a lightly floured surface, roll out half of the pastry dough to about ⅛ inch. Lift and drape over a 9-inch pie pan. Do not trim the sides. Freeze or chill for 20 minutes.

2. Combine the flour, cornstarch, the ¼ cup sugar, and the cinnamon in a large bowl. Stir in the crème fraîche. Add the blueberries (frozen if the pie is to be frozen) and pear, and toss to mix. Pile into the chilled piecrust. Brush the pastry rim with water.

3. Roll out the remaining pastry to ¼ inch thick. Cut the pastry into 1-inch-wide, 10-inch-long strips—use a pasta wheel for a fluted edge, if you like. You will need at least nine strips. Arrange the strips in a lattice pattern, weaving where needed, and leaving holes for the filling to show through. Trim the ends and press pastry all round to secure. Chill or freeze for 20 minutes.

4. Preheat the oven to 400°F. Place a rack in the center of the oven and place a baking sheet on it to preheat.

5. Brush the chilled pie with the egg glaze and sprinkle with sugar. Place on the preheated baking sheet and bake for 50 minutes or until golden brown and crisp and the filling is bubbling. Allow to cool for 10 minutes before serving.

To freeze: Remember to use frozen blueberries. Freeze the unbaked pie once assembled, but do not glaze. Freeze for 2 hours or until solid. Wrap the surface with plastic freezer wrap followed by heavy-duty foil. If intending to freeze longer than 3 days, remove from the pie pan. Wrap in plastic freezer wrap followed by heavy-duty foil.

To bake: Bake straight from the freezer. Preheat the oven to 400°F. Place the rack in the center of the oven. Place a baking sheet in the oven to preheat. Remove the wrapping from the pie and if necessary return to the pie pan. Brush the pastry with egg glaze and sprinkle with sugar. Place on the preheated baking sheet, and bake for 50 minutes. Cover with foil and continue to bake for an additional 30 minutes or until the filling is bubbling and the crust is crisp and golden.

Apple Strudel

For an alternative filling, use ripe Bosc pears in place of the apples and replace the almonds with walnuts. In place of raisins, chopped dates will be perfect. Serve the strudel with a blue cheese such as Roquefort or a cream dolcelatte.

6 tablespoons unsalted butter

¼ cup fresh fine bread crumbs

2 tablespoons sliced almonds

1 pound Granny Smith apples

Grated zest and juice from 1 lemon

3 tablespoons golden raisins

½ teaspoon ground cinnamon

2 tablespoons granulated sugar

Five 12 × 16-inch phyllo pastry
   sheets, thawed if frozen
   (see page 132 for tips)

2 tablespoons confectioners' sugar

SERVES 6

FREEZE FOR UP TO 1 MONTH

1. Melt 2 tablespoons of the butter in a skillet over low heat. Add the bread crumbs and cook for 8 to 10 minutes until crisp and golden brown. Stir frequently to break up any clumps. Transfer to a paper-towel-lined plate.

2. Meanwhile, heat another tablespoon of the butter in a small skillet and sauté the almonds over low heat for 4 minutes or until golden brown. Transfer to a paper-towel-lined plate.

3. Peel and core the apples. Slice the apples into ¼-inch-thick wedges. Place the apples in a large bowl and add the lemon zest and juice, raisins, cinnamon, and granulated sugar. Toss to coat. Melt the remaining butter and set aside.

4. Preheat the oven to 375°F. Place a rack in the center of the oven. Line a baking sheet with parchment paper.

5. Unroll the phyllo pastry and drape with plastic wrap to keep damp. Place a clean kitchen towel in front of you and place one sheet of pastry on top horizontally. Sift over with a light dusting of confectioners' sugar. Lay a sheet of phyllo over the sugar and brush with some melted butter. Add one more sheet on top and brush

with more butter. Sprinkle the lower third of the pastry with a third of the bread crumb mixture. Place another two sheets of pastry on top, brushing with butter between them. Sprinkle another third of the bread crumb mixture over the lower third of the pastry. Spread the apple filling on top of the bread crumbs, leaving a 4-inch margin on both shorter ends. Sprinkle the almonds on top of the apples.

6. Lift the two shorter ends of the pastry up over the apple filling. Using the towel, start to roll from the apple-filled part of the phyllo. Roll the strudel halfway. Sprinkle the pastry with the remaining bread crumb mixture. Finish rolling and transfer to the prepared baking sheet. Brush the pastry with the remaining butter.

7. Bake for 40 minutes or until golden brown on the top and bottom. Allow to cool for 10 minutes. Dust with the remaining confectioners' sugar and serve.

To freeze: Do not bake the strudel. Place on a baking sheet lined with plastic wrap and freeze until solid, about 2 hours. Wrap in plastic freezer wrap followed by heavy-duty foil.

To bake: Bake straight from the freezer. Preheat the oven to 375°F. Place a rack in the center of the oven. Remove the foil and plastic wrap from the strudel and place on a baking sheet lined with parchment paper. Bake for 50 minutes, covering loosely with foil halfway through. Cool for 10 minutes before serving. Dust with extra confectioners' sugar to serve.

Chocolate Profiteroles

The filled profiteroles can be frozen if you are using choux buns that have not already been frozen. If you intend to freeze the filled choux buns, make the sauce on the day required, as that cannot be frozen.

The fillings can be varied for the choux buns—whisk a tablespoon of vanilla or orange liqueur into the cream. Feel free to use your favorite ice cream flavor, either chocolate or coffee.

For a mocha sauce, substitute ½ cup freshly brewed espresso coffee for ½ cup water.

SAUCE

8 ounces bittersweet chocolate

¼ cup sugar

1 tablespoon honey

32 choux buns, thawed if frozen

(page 138)

FILLING

1 pint softened vanilla ice cream

or

1½ cups heavy cream whipped

with 2 tablespoons sugar and

1 teaspoon pure vanilla extract

MAKES 32 TO 34

FREEZE FOR UP TO 2 WEEKS

1. To prepare the sauce, put the chocolate, sugar, and honey into a small pot with $\frac{3}{4}$ cup water and cook over low heat for 5 to 8 minutes until the chocolate melts into the remaining ingredients. Stir frequently until smooth.

2. To fill the choux buns with ice cream, make a small insertion on the side of each bun, open up slightly, and spoon in about 1 heaping teaspoon of ice cream. If planning to fill with whipped cream, spoon the whipped cream into a piping bag fitted with a ¼-inch plain piping nozzle. Pipe the whipped cream into the buns through the small hole made earlier to allow steam to escape the buns on baking. Serve the profiteroles immediately with the chocolate sauce alongside.

To freeze: Once the unfilled choux buns have cooled, place them on a baking sheet, leaving about 1 inch between them. Open freeze until solid, about 1 hour. Slit the profiteroles slightly and fill with softened ice cream. Return to the freezer for about 1 hour. Place in an airtight freezer-safe container and freeze. Do not freeze the sauce.

To thaw: Remove the required amount of ice cream–filled profiteroles from the freezer and allow to stand in the fridge while making the sauce. This will allow the ice cream to soften slightly. Make the sauce on the day required.

sweets

At the end of a dinner party, it's amazing how everyone's eyes light up when a homemade ice cream, cake, or chocolate creation is served. Getting this reaction need not be hard work. With the help of a good ice cream maker it's no effort at all to experiment with sorbets and ice creams. Try using different fruits, extracts, and herbs for varying flavors. To make granitas, no special equipment is required except for a fork! If you're short on time, pick up a pint of your favorite premium store-bought ice cream or sorbet for a quick and easy alternative. Use the ice cream or sorbet between layers of sponge cake before freezing. Cut the assembled cake into bars or squares and you have a fantastic homemade dessert. Icebox cookies, crunchy meringues, or a chocolate terrine, all featured in this chapter, also hold up well in the freezer and can be served on a few moments' notice when company calls.

Sticky Toffee Pudding

This traditional English dessert is less of a pudding and more of steamed date sponge cake surrounded by toffee caramel sauce. The pudding is frozen uncooked and steamed straight from the freezer.

SAUCE

1 cup sugar

1 cup heavy cream

PUDDING

8 ounces Medjool dates, pitted and
   chopped

2 teaspoons baking soda

$^3/_4$ cup light brown sugar

8 tablespoons (1 stick) unsalted
   butter, softened

1 teaspoon pure vanilla extract

1 large egg, beaten

2$^1/_3$ cups cake flour

1 teaspoon baking powder

MAKES 8 INDIVIDUAL PUDDINGS

FREEZE FOR UP TO 1 MONTH

1. Rub the sides and bases of eight 6-ounce ramekins, ovenproof glass bowls, or individual heavy foil tins with a little soft butter. Line the bottoms with parchment paper and butter the parchment. Set aside.

2. To prepare the toffee sauce, put the sugar and $^3/_4$ cup water in a heavy-bottomed pot and cook over low heat, stirring occasionally, until the sugar dissolves. Increase the heat until the mixture comes to a boil. Boil steadily for 15 minutes or until a deep amber caramel is formed. Remove the caramel from the heat and allow to cool for 1 minute. Stir in the cream and return to a boil. Cool for 10 minutes, then pour the sauce evenly into the prepared ramekins, allowing about $^1/_2$ inch of sauce per cup. Allow to cool and set a little.

3. Preheat the oven to 400°F. Place a rack in the middle of the oven. (Do not preheat the oven if you plan to freeze the puddings.)

4. Put the chopped dates in a clean pot with 1 cup water and gently bring to a boil. Remove from the heat and mix in the baking soda. Set aside.

> *continued*

5. Beat the sugar and butter in a large mixing bowl until light and creamy. Gradually beat in the vanilla and egg. Sift together the cake flour and baking powder into a bowl and fold into the sugar and egg. Stir in the date mixture.

6. Divide the cake mixture among the ramekins, filling each to about ½ inch below the top. Cover the top with a disc of waxed paper.

7. To steam the puddings, place a wire rack inside a large roasting pan. Add an inch of hot water and place the ramekins on the rack. Cover the pan loosely with heavy-duty foil. Place in the oven and steam for 45 minutes. The cake will have risen and a skewer inserted into the cake part of the pudding should come out clean. Transfer the puddings to a separate cooling rack. Allow to cool for 5 minutes. Run a small knife around the edge of the cake to loosen. Turn out onto individual serving plates. Serve immediately with the sauce dripping down the sides of the cake.

To freeze: Cover the assembled, uncooked puddings (sauce and cake mixture) with a disc of waxed paper. Place in the freezer until solid, about 2 hours. Once the puddings are frozen solid, cover them with a lid or tightly with heavy-duty foil. Stack in the freezer.

To cook: Cook straight from the freezer. Preheat the oven to 375°F. Place a rack in the middle of the oven and set up an "oven-steamer" as described above. Add the puddings, removing the lids or foil covers. Cover the steamer loosely with heavy-duty foil and bake for 1 hour or until well risen and a skewer comes out clean. Transfer the puddings to a cooling rack and leave to stand for 5 minutes. Run a knife around the edge to loosen. Turn out to serve.

Layered Coconut Cake

When I first tried a slice of this cake in Charleston, South Carolina, it had about eight layers and looked perfect. It took all of my willpower not to make a spectacle of myself and order a second slice.

A sponge cake freezes exceptionally well—freeze the sponge cake separately and assemble on the day required, or freeze the whole finished thing. It will take up quite a bit of space in the freezer.

CAKE

2½ cups cake flour

2 teaspoons baking powder

¼ teaspoon fine salt

1 cup milk, at room temperature

1 teaspoon pure vanilla extract

6 ounces (1½ sticks) unsalted
   butter, at room temperature

1½ cups superfine sugar

3 large eggs, at room temperature,
   beaten

SERVES 8 TO 10

FREEZE FOR UP TO
1 WEEK IF ASSEMBLED

FREEZE FOR UP TO
2 WEEKS WITHOUT FILLING,
FROSTING, AND COCONUT

1. Preheat the oven to 350°F. Place a rack in the center of the oven. Lightly grease the bottom and sides of two 8-inch cake pans. Line the bottoms with parchment paper and grease the paper.

2. To prepare the cake, sift the flour, baking powder, and salt into a bowl and set aside. Combine the milk and vanilla in a small bowl and set aside. Place the butter in a mixing bowl and beat with a handheld electric mixer (use a paddle beater if using a large standup mixer) on medium speed until soft. Add the sugar and continue to beat for 4 to 5 minutes until light and creamy. Gradually add the eggs one at a time, beating well between each addition, and stopping occasionally to scrape down the sides of the bowl. Reduce the speed to low and add the flour and milk mixtures, alternately, in four batches, starting with the flour. If using a handheld electric mixer, fold the flour and milk mixtures by hand using a rubber spatula.

> *continued*

FILLING

³/₄ cup sugar

¼ cup cornstarch

1¼ cups canned unsweetened
coconut milk

Juice from ½ lemon

2 large eggs, beaten

3 tablespoons unsalted butter,
chilled

FROSTING

1½ cups heavy cream, chilled

¼ cup confectioners' sugar

2½ cups sweetened shredded
coconut or fresh shredded
coconut (see page 20)

3. Divide the batter between the prepared cake pans and spread with a spatula, going from center to sides, allowing the sides to be a little higher. This will help ensure level rising. Bake for 30 to 35 minutes until the top of the cake springs back when gently pressed and the sides just pull away from the pan.

4. Place the cake pans on a cooling rack and let stand for 5 to 10 minutes. Turn out the cakes, peel back the parchment paper from the cakes, and put them back on the cake very lightly. (The parchment will stick to the cake and make it soggy if left to cool tightly on the cake.) Invert the cake once more on another cooling rack so the tops are facing up (the parchment on the base will prevent the cake from sticking to the cake rack). Let sit until fully cooled.

5. To prepare the filling, mix the sugar and cornstarch in a small pot. Gradually stir in the coconut milk and lemon juice. Bring to a boil over moderate heat, whisking constantly. Continue to cook for 2 minutes or until glossy and thick. Whisk half of the coconut mixture into the eggs, then return the mixture to the pot. Cook for 2 minutes or until the mixture boils. Remove from the heat and whisk in the chilled butter, 1 tablespoon at a time. Transfer to a bowl and cover the surface directly with plastic wrap to prevent a skin from forming. Refrigerate for at least 30 minutes or overnight.

6. To assemble the cake, horizontally slice each cake with a serrated knife, to create four halves. Place one layer on a clean surface and spread with a third of the filling. Repeat with the remaining layers, finishing with a layer of cake on top.

7. To prepare the frosting, whip the chilled cream for 2 minutes or until soft peaks form. Sift in the sugar and continue to whip until stiff peaks form. Spread the whipped cream over the top and sides of the cake in an even thin layer. Sprinkle the sides and top with the shredded coconut. With a large, wide spatula, transfer to a clean baking sheet or cake plate and chill in the refrigerator for at least 1 hour before required.

To freeze: To freeze the unfilled sponge cakes, place cooled, room temperature layers on a baking sheet lined with plastic wrap. Open freeze until solid, about 1 hour. Working quickly, wrap the layers with plastic freezer wrap, then foil. Label and freeze for up to 2 weeks.

To freeze the assembled and frosted cake, place on a baking sheet lined with waxed paper. Open freeze until solid, about 4 hours. Remove from the freezer and cover with plastic freezer wrap followed by foil. Return to the freezer.

To thaw: To thaw the sponge cakes, remove the foil and plastic wrap from each cake. Rewrap immediately with new plastic wrap and leave at room temperature for 2 hours to thaw. Once thawed place in an airtight container. Assemble within 2 days.

To thaw the assembled cake, remove from the freezer and remove the foil and plastic wrap. Place on a flat plate or cake stand and thaw for at least 2 hours in the fridge. The cake may be stored for up to 48 hours in the fridge.

Chocolate Truffle Terrine

This terrine can be prepared and served without freezing. Just chill the completed dessert for at least three hours to set. Turn out and serve with berries. Store any leftover terrine in the freezer.

1 pound bittersweet chocolate, finely chopped

2 cups heavy cream

3 tablespoons rum or cognac

1 cup shelled pistachios, finely chopped

Cocoa powder for dusting

Coffee ice cream for serving

SERVES 10

FREEZE FOR UP TO 1 MONTH

1. Line the base of a 9 × 4-inch loaf pan or terrine, preferably one with collapsible sides, with parchment paper.

2. Place the chocolate in a heatproof bowl over a pan of simmering water until melted and smooth, stirring frequently. Allow the chocolate to cool slightly.

3. Meanwhile, whisk the cream and cognac in a bowl until the mixture just leaves a trail on the surface when the whisk is lifted. Do not whisk until too thick.

4. Fold half of the melted chocolate into the cream mixture, using a plastic spatula. Once thoroughly combined, add the remaining chocolate and fold in. Pour a third of the mixture into the prepared pan and sprinkle with half of the chopped pistachios in an even layer. Freeze for 10 minutes to set slightly (keep the remaining truffle mixture covered with plastic wrap). Add another third of the chocolate mixture to the terrine and sprinkle with the remaining pistachios. Freeze once more for 10 minutes to set the surface slightly. Add the remaining chocolate mixture and spread evenly. If making to serve that day, allow the terrine to chill for 3 hours until set.

5. To remove from the pan to serve, run a hot, thin-bladed knife around the sides of the loaf pan and turn out onto a serving plate or board. If using a loaf pan with collapsible sides, loosen the sides as above, and gently ease the sides of the pan down. Invert onto a serving plate. Dust the terrine with cocoa powder. Cut the terrine into ½-inch slices and serve with coffee ice cream.

To freeze: Once assembled, freeze the terrine until solid, about 2 hours. Remove from the pan and cover first with plastic freezer wrap, then heavy-duty foil.

To thaw: Remove the terrine from the freezer and remove the foil and plastic wrap. Place the terrine on a serving plate and allow to stand at room temperature for 1 hour.

Chocolate Chunk Cookies

Two rules apply when it comes to making these amazing melting cookies. First, the dough must be beaten for a full 10 minutes. Second, the dough must be well chilled before baking; otherwise it will spread too thinly, giving way to a crisp rather than a chewy cookie. A quick tip—one of the easiest ways to chop chocolate is to use a serrated bread knife.

1¼ cups all-purpose flour

¼ teaspoon baking soda

Pinch of fine salt

8 tablespoons (1 stick) unsalted
butter, softened

½ cup soft light brown sugar

¼ cup superfine sugar

1 large egg, beaten

1 teaspoon pure vanilla extract

10 ounces milk, semisweet, or
bittersweet chocolate, coarsely
chopped

MAKES 22 COOKIES

FREEZE FOR UP TO 2 WEEKS

1. Sift the flour, baking soda, and salt into a bowl and set aside. Beat the butter with a handheld electric mixer (use a paddle beater if using a large standup mixer) until smooth. Add the sugars and beat until light and creamy. Gradually beat in the egg, followed by the vanilla. Once combined, continue beating the mixture for 10 minutes, continuing to scrape down the sides of the bowl. The batter will become very light in color.

2. Gradually fold the flour mixture into the batter. Add the chocolate chunks. Cover the dough in the bowl and chill for at least 30 minutes. Shape the dough into about twenty-two 1½-inch balls. Refrigerate for at least 1 hour.

3. Preheat the oven to 300°F. Place a rack in the center of the oven. Line two baking sheets with parchment paper.

4. Arrange six to eight cookies on each baking sheet. Bake for 10 to 15 minutes until the surface is no longer glossy. The dough may look slightly underdone; however, the bottoms of the cookies should be just golden. Using a metal spatula, carefully transfer the cookies to a rack and let cool. Continue baking the remaining cookies. Store the baked cookies in an airtight container for up to 3 days.

To freeze: Line a baking sheet with plastic wrap. Arrange the uncooked cookie balls (no need to refrigerate) on the baking sheet, leaving about 1 inch between them. Open freeze until solid, about 1 hour. Transfer the balls to a plastic freezer bag and seal tightly, removing as much excess air as possible. Alternatively, pack in a freezer-safe plastic container.

To cook: Bake the cookie dough balls straight from the freezer. Preheat the oven to 350°F. Place six to eight cookie balls on a parchment-lined baking sheet and bake for 20 minutes or until the surface is no longer glossy.

Icebox Cookies

Keep this cookie dough in the freezer to have on hand for a quick easy dessert. Serve the cookies as a petit four with after-dinner coffee. The fennel seed cookies (see Variations) make a wonderful accompaniment to wine and cheese.

2 cups all-purpose flour

Pinch of fine salt

Pinch of ground cinnamon

12 tablespoons (1½ sticks)
   unsalted butter, at room
   temperature

¾ cup granulated sugar

1 large egg yolk

1 teaspoon pure vanilla extract

¼ cup Demerara or raw sugar

MAKES 48

FREEZE FOR UP TO 1 MONTH

1. Sift the flour, salt, and cinnamon into a bowl. Place the butter in the bowl of a standing mixer fitted with a paddle beater. Mix until smooth. Add the granulated sugar, egg yolk, and vanilla; beat until light but not airy. Set the mixer on low speed and gradually add the flour, scraping down the sides of the bowl. The mixture should be just combined. Divide the dough in half. Roll each half into a ball, cover with plastic wrap, and refrigerate for 30 minutes.

2. Knead the cookie dough gently and roll each half into a log 1½ inches thick and 7 inches long. Freeze.

To freeze: Wrap in waxed paper or parchment paper, trying to keep the shape smooth. Freeze for 15 minutes, then roll a little between your hands to make sure the log is round without a flattened circumference. Freeze for another 30 minutes or until the logs are solid. Remove the paper and wrap with plastic freezer wrap, then heavy-duty foil. Freeze until required.

> *continued*

To cook: Cook from frozen. Preheat the oven to 350°F. Line a baking sheet with parchment paper. Unwrap the cookie dough and allow to stand at room temperature for 5 minutes. Using a thin-bladed knife, cut the cookie dough into $1/4$-inch-thick slices and place on a baking sheet about 1 inch apart. Bake for 12 minutes. The cookies should be golden brown on the bottom but still very pale on the top. Cool on a cake rack.

VARIATIONS

Chocolate and Hazelnut: Replace $1/2$ cup of the flour with cocoa powder and add $1/2$ cup skinned, chopped hazelnuts. Omit the cinnamon. Bake for 15 minutes.

Lemon and Rosemary: Replace the cinnamon and vanilla with the grated zest of 1 lemon and 1 teaspoon finely chopped fresh rosemary.

Coffee: Add 2 tablespoons medium ground fresh coffee to the butter and sugar mixture. Omit the cinnamon.

Orange and Cumin: Add the grated zest from 1 orange to the butter and sugar mixture. Replace the cinnamon and vanilla with $1/4$ teaspoon ground cumin.

Fennel Seed: Place 1 teaspoon fennel seeds in a mortar and lightly crush with a pestle. Use to replace the cinnamon.

Meringues

Having frozen meringues on hand means that you don't have to worry about making them on humid days when they won't hold together. Served from the freezer, the meringues remain crisp and crunchy. If you prefer your meringues crunchy on the outside and chewy in the center, then thaw them at room temperature for two hours before serving.

MAKES 20 MERINGUES

FREEZE FOR UP TO 2 WEEKS

3 large egg whites, at room

    temperature

1¼ cups superfine sugar

1. Preheat the oven to 275°F. Line two baking sheets with waxed paper or parchment paper.

2. Place the egg whites and sugar in a large heatproof bowl. Place the bowl over a pan of barely simmering water—do not allow the bowl to touch the water. Stir until the sugar dissolves. Using an electric handheld mixer, whisk until stiff peaks form, 4 to 5 minutes. Remove the bowl from the pan and continue to whisk until the mixture is smooth, glossy, and very peaky.

3. Spoon large spoonfuls of swirls at least 2 inches apart on the prepared baking sheets. Bake for 40 minutes or until dry but still just soft in the center. Place the baking sheets on cooling racks and let stand until completely cooled (if the weather is hot and humid, turn off the oven, leave the door slightly ajar, and leave to cool for at least 2 hours).

To freeze: Place the meringues on one to two baking sheets lined with waxed paper and open freeze for 1 hour or until solid. Pack in freezer-safe plastic containers, cover, and freeze until required.

To serve: Either serve straight from the freezer for a crunchy, dry meringue or thaw for 2 hours at room temperature for a meringue with a soft chewy center and crunchy outside.

> *continued*

For an instant dessert, roughly crush meringues into large pieces and serve with macerated berries (with 1 to 2 tablespoons honey and fresh mint) and freshly whipped cream. Crushed meringues can also be a topping on ice cream sundaes.

VARIATIONS

Chocolate Marble: Melt 3 ounces chopped bittersweet chocolate in a heatproof bowl set over a pan of simmering water. Allow to cool and fold into the whisked meringues. Bake for 2 hours at 225°F.

Nuts: Fold ³/₄ cup chopped almonds or hazelnuts into the meringue before spooning onto the baking sheet.

Meringue Gâteau: Instead of making individual meringues, mark out three 7-inch circles on parchment paper and place on three baking sheets, marked side down. Spread the meringue just inside the circle, as the meringue will expand on baking. Bake for 40 minutes or until dry. Let cool. Open freeze until solid, then gently cover with plastic freezer wrap and then heavy-duty foil. To assemble, remove from the freezer and sandwich with 1 cup chilled heavy cream whipped with 2 tablespoons confectioners' sugar and vanilla seeds scraped from 1 vanilla bean. Scatter 1 pint raspberries on the top layer. Chill for 1 hour before required. Dust with confectioners' sugar to serve.

Strawberry Ice Cream and Raspberry Sorbet Bars

To cut down on time, feel free to use your favorite store-bought ice cream and sorbet. If you prefer, the bars can be cut prior to serving and wrapped individually in waxed paper, with the ends twisted to serve like bonbons; cover with foil while stored in the freezer.

CAKE

1½ cups cake flour

½ teaspoon baking powder

¼ teaspoon baking soda

¼ teaspoon fine salt

2 large eggs, at room temperature

1 teaspoon pure vanilla extract

5 tablespoons unsalted butter,
   at room temperature

³/₄ cup sugar

½ cup buttermilk, at room
   temperature

MAKES 16 BARS

FREEZE FOR UP TO 2 WEEKS

1. Preheat the oven to 350°F. Lightly grease and line the bottom of a 9-inch square cake pan with parchment paper. Grease the top of the parchment paper.

2. To prepare the cake, sift the flour, baking powder, baking soda, and salt into a bowl and set aside. Combine the eggs and vanilla in a small bowl and set aside. Beat the butter with a handheld electric mixer (use a paddle beater if using a large standup mixer) until smooth. Add the sugar and beat for 4 minutes or until the mixture is light and creamy. Gradually beat in the egg mixture. Using a large metal spoon or large rubber spatula, alternately fold in the flour and buttermilk in four batches, mixing well between each addition.

3. Spoon the batter into the prepared cake pan, leveling the surface and making a slight dip in the center. Bake for 20 to 25 minutes until golden and the cake shrinks back slightly from the sides of the pan. Let stand for 10 minutes before turning out onto a rack. Let the cake cool completely.

1 cup milk

3 egg yolks

½ cup sugar

1½ pints strawberries, washed,
    hulled, and coarsely chopped

1 cup heavy cream, chilled

SORBET

1 cup sugar

¼ cup corn syrup

2 mint sprigs

2 pints raspberries

4. To prepare the ice cream, heat the milk in a small pot. Place the eggs and sugar in a bowl and whisk. Pour in the warm milk, whisking until the sugar dissolves. Return the mixture to the pan. Cook over low heat for 5 minutes, stirring constantly until the custard thickens enough to coat the back of a spoon. Do not allow the mixture to boil. Pour into a bowl. Cover the surface directly with plastic wrap to prevent a skin from forming. Let cool to room temperature.

5. Puree the strawberries in a blender. Strain the puree through a fine sieve, discarding any seeds or large chunks. Stir the puree into the cooled custard. Chill for 1 hour. In a clean bowl, whisk the cream until very soft peaks form. Fold into the strawberry custard mixture. Transfer to an ice cream machine and churn according to the manufacturer's instructions, about 25 minutes, depending on the machine. Freeze until required—but not solid.

6. To prepare the sorbet, place 1 cup water, the sugar, and corn syrup in a pot and cook over low heat, stirring until the sugar dissolves. Increase the heat, bring to a boil, and boil for 3 minutes or until just syrupy. Add the mint. Transfer the mixture to a bowl and let cool completely.

> *continued*

7. Place the raspberries in a blender and puree. Strain through a sieve and discard any seeds or large chunks. Add the raspberries to the syrup and mix to combine. Discard the mint. Refrigerate for 1 hour. Churn in an ice cream machine according to the manufacturer's instructions until thick, about 25 minutes. Transfer to a container and freeze until required.

8. Once the ice cream and sorbet are prepared, clean the cake pan and line the sides and bottom with plastic wrap. Use a serrated knife to slice the cake in half horizontally. Return one half to the prepared pan, cut side up. Spread half of the ice cream on top and freeze for 20 minutes if too soft. Spread half of the sorbet on top of the ice cream and freeze until just set if needed, about 30 minutes. Continue the layers, finishing with the sorbet and then the cake. Cover the surface of the cake with plastic wrap, then foil. Freeze for 2 hours or overnight.

9. To serve, turn out onto a chopping board, remove the plastic wrap, and leave in the fridge (or at room temperature) for 20 minutes. For bars, cut the cake into 1½-inch-thick slices, then cut crosswise into 1½-inch-thick bars. Serve or rewrap and freeze until required.

Iced Zabaglione Soufflés

These soufflés contain a high sugar content that allows them to take on a semifreddo consistency when frozen (which means that they will never set hard). If you do not want to set each soufflé individually, simply fold in the crushed amaretto cookies and freeze in a freezer-safe plastic container for at least three hours and serve in scoops.

4 large eggs, separated

1½ cups sugar

½ cup sweet Marsala

1 cup heavy cream

1 cup lightly crushed amaretto
  cookies

Almond praline to serve
  (see Note on page 198)

MAKES 8

FREEZE FOR UP TO 4 DAYS

1. Put eight ⅓-cup (3-ounce) sundae/parfait glasses on a baking sheet and freeze until required. Cut out eight strips of waxed paper, about 10 inches long and 3 inches wide, and set aside. Fill a large bowl with ice and water and set aside.

2. Place the egg yolks and ¼ cup of the sugar in a heatproof bowl and beat with a handheld electric mixer until pale and thick. Add the Marsala and mix well. Place the bowl over a pan of simmering water and whisk for 12 to 15 minutes; the mixture should be thick and ribbonlike when the beaters are lifted. Remove from the heat and quickly set the base of the bowl in the bowl of prepared ice cold water. Set aside to cool.

3. To prepare the meringue, place the egg whites in a bowl. Place the remaining sugar in a small pot with ½ cup water and cook over low heat, stirring until the sugar dissolves. Increase the heat. When the syrup comes to 240°F, start to whisk the egg whites with an electric mixer fitted with a wisk. By the time the syrup comes to 250°F, soft peaks should have formed with the egg whites; start to add the syrup to the egg whites in a thin steady stream. Continue whisking until the mixture is tepid. The meringue should be thick and glossy.

> *continued*

4. In a separate bowl, whisk the cream until soft peaks form. Using a large metal spoon or rubber spatula, fold the cream into the custard mixture. Fold in the meringue.

5. Divide the crushed amaretto cookies evenly among the chilled glasses. Spoon the zabaglione mixture on top, right up to the rim. Take a strip of cut waxed paper, and wrap around the glass (the condensation from chilling will allow the paper to stick to the side of the sundae glass). The paper should come 2 inches above the rim of the glass. Spoon more of the zabaglione mixture to come above the rim. Level the surface. Return to the freezer to set, about 3 hours or overnight. Cover the surface with plastic freezer wrap once set.

6. To serve, gently peel away the waxed paper collar and plastic wrap if used. Serve with almond praline.

Note: To make quick almond praline: Dissolve 1 cup sugar in $1/2$ cup water in a saucepan over low heat. Bring to a boil and cook for 10 to 15 minutes until a deep amber caramel is formed. Stir in $1/2$ cup lightly toasted sliced almonds and pour the mixture onto an oiled baking sheet. Leave to set, about 30 minutes.

Break in large pieces to serve. The almond praline can be stored in an airtight container in the fridge or freezer for 3 days (crushed praline can be stored in the freezer for up to 3 weeks).

Granitas

Granitas make an elegantly light and refreshing end to a dinner party—especially the coffee and lemon verbena variations. The fruit variety makes for a delicious summer cocktail.

The secret to a successful granita is to add a little alcohol, as it does not freeze; therefore you can form light, delicate flakes of ice instead of heavy clumps of ice. If you don't want to match the fruit with a specific liqueur, vodka or grappa are neutral and will not give an aftertaste.

Other herbs that can be used are mint and basil (especially Thai basil). Orange blossom and rose water also make fragrant additions to fruit granitas.

MAKES 1 QUART

FREEZE FOR UP TO 2 WEEKS

COFFEE

1 cup light brown sugar or grated

    palm sugar

2 cups freshly made espresso

2 tablespoons brandy

PASSION FRUIT

12 passion fruit

²/₃ cups sugar

2 tablespoons grappa

LEMON VERBENA

1 cup sugar

3 lemon verbena sprigs

3 strips lemon zest, each about

    3 inches long

Juice of 2 lemons

2 tablespoons sweet white wine

1. **COFFEE:** Dissolve the sugar in the coffee and stir in the brandy. Chill for 1 hour.

1. **PASSION FRUIT:** Halve the passion fruit and strain through a sieve, discarding the seeds. You should be left with ⅔ cup juice. Place 2 cups water and the sugar in a small pot and cook over low heat, stirring until the sugar dissolves. Increase the heat, bring the mixture to a boil, and cook for 5 minutes or until a light syrup forms. Pour the syrup into a bowl and stir in the grappa and passion fruit juice until well combined. Allow the mixture to come to room temperature, then refrigerate for 1 hour.

1. **LEMON VERBENA:** Place 2 cups water, the sugar, lemon verbena, and lemon zest in a small pot and cook over low heat, stirring until the sugar dissolves. Increase the heat, bring the mixture to a boil, and boil for 5 minutes or until light syrup forms. Pour the syrup into a bowl and stir in the lemon juice and white wine until well combined. Allow to cool to room temperature, then chill in the refrigerator for 1 hour. Chill. Strain to remove and discard the flavorings.

2. Once the mixture for the granita has chilled, transfer to a 1-quart freezer-safe plastic container. Freeze for up to 4 hours, stirring with a fork every hour (scraping the sides into the center, as they freeze faster than the center) to create small fine crystal-like flakes. By the third stirring, you will notice the granita increase in volume. Freeze for at least 2 hours after the granita is complete. Serve in chilled glasses.

Tropical Fruit Sorbet Popsicles

These Popsicles are the perfect refresher for a summer barbecue. Full of fruit flavor, they are ideal for children and adults alike. For a more sophisticated treat, omit the Popsicle sticks and serve a few scoops of the sorbet in chilled cocktail glasses.

²/₃ cup sugar

5 ripe mangos, peeled and flesh
   cut away from the pit

or

4 pounds seedless watermelon,
   cut into chunks

or

3 pounds ripe papaya, seeds and
   skin removed

Juice of 2 limes

**MAKES 12 POPSICLES OR
1½ QUARTS SORBET
FREEZE FOR UP TO 2 WEEKS**

1. Place twelve ⅓-cup (3-ounce) plastic cups on a baking sheet and place in the freezer.

2. Place 2 cups water and the sugar in a small pot and cook over low heat, stirring until the sugar dissolves. Bring to a boil and cook for 5 minutes or until a light syrup forms. Pour the syrup into a bowl and set aside to cool to room temperature.

3. Place the fruit in a blender (a food processor will give a different texture)—you may need to do this in two batches—and puree. Strain the puree through a sieve to remove any seeds or large lumps. Mix the fruit puree with the cooled syrup and stir in the lime juice until well combined. Refrigerate for 1 hour.

4. Place the fruit puree in an ice cream machine and churn for 30 to 40 minutes or according to the manufacturer's instructions. Once the sorbet is thick, spoon it into the chilled cups and insert a Popsicle stick in the center. Freeze for 2 hours or until solid. To store, place all of the Popsicles in a freezer-safe plastic container with a tight-fitting lid.

5. To remove the plastic cup, hold the cup in the palm of your hand for 30 seconds, then gently ease the cup away from the Popsicle. Serve.

glossary

Aleppo pepper: A sharp, sweet chile from Aleppo, Syria. It has a fruity flavor that allows the final taste to be light with an almost fragrant kick. Deep, rich red in color, Aleppo pepper looks particularly appetizing on grilled meats and chicken and roasted vegetables. Red pepper flakes can be substituted.

Black rice vinegar: The balsamic vinegar of Asian cooking. Its quality, like balsamic, depends on how long the vinegar has been allowed to ferment. Black rice vinegar has a rich, deep flavor with no sourness. It is sharp and mellow, but not sweet like balsamic. Use in small quantities mixed with garlic, ginger, a sprinkling of sugar, and a little lime juice as a salad dressing or as a dip for dumplings.

Cracked olives: Raw green olives are smashed so the flesh is broken in places, then placed in brine and spices for several weeks. The olives are sold in jars or at olive bars, seasoned with chiles and lemons, or with olive oil, garlic, and oregano.

Demi-glace: A concentrated brown glaze made from a veal stock and sherry or Madeira. It can be made at home, but why bother when quality demi-glace is sold in plastic resealable containers in the frozen food section of supermarkets and gourmet shops.

Dumpling wrappers: You can use dumpling wrappers or wonton wrappers for the Gyoza (page 54). Two main differences—the Japanese gyoza use a round-shaped wrapper made without eggs. Wonton wrappers are usually made with eggs and are available round or square. They are available fresh or frozen in all Asian markets and many supermarkets.

Fermented black beans: Also known as salted black beans. These are fermented soybeans preserved in salt and spices. Use in marinades with ginger and garlic for stir-fries. It's up to you to rinse or not—it depends on how much of their characteristic flavor you want. Excellent with seafood, chicken, or beef.

Garlic, mashed: Smash the garlic clove and then discard the paper skin. Sprinkle the garlic with ½ teaspoon sea salt or kosher salt. Use the side of a thin-bladed knife to mash until smooth. Use mashed garlic in salad dressings, soups, and sauces.

Garlic, smashed: When you bash a garlic clove with the flat side of a knife, the skin splits to expose the clove. The garlic clove is added to the dish with the paper skin still on. Use in marinades, roasting, stews, or braising.

Mirin: A sweet rice wine used in Japanese cooking. Excellent in glazes, salad dressings, and sauces. Available in all Asian markets and many supermarkets.

Miso: A thick paste made from soybeans fermented with sea salt and *koji*—the latter a product made of fermenting rice, barley, or soybeans with a mold culture. Commonly used in Japanese cooking, miso is available white, brown, or red. Use in marinades for barbecue sauces. Add a teaspoon when making salad dressings. The paste is available from health food shops and Asian markets in the produce section. Keep stored in the refrigerator for up to 3 months, before and after opening.

Pepitas: Hulled pumpkin seeds. These are good for snacking, but also in the Mexican Chickpea Stew with Green Salsa (page 107). Use the unroasted and unsalted variety.

Preserved lemons: Lemons are preserved in a salt–lemon juice mixture, often with cinnamon sticks, whole cloves, or coriander seeds thrown in as well. Popular in North African and Middle Eastern cooking, they add a fragrant lemon tang to finished foods. Remove the lemons from their brine and soak them for about 30 minutes in water to get rid of excess salt. They can be finely chopped or sliced, and used in chicken, fish, or seafood salads. You'll find them in North African and Middle Eastern spice shops.

Sambal oelek: A Thai paste made with hot chiles that is good in marinades, rubs, and dipping sauces. The Vietnamese version, made with chiles and garlic paste, is also referred to as sambal oelek by some manufacturers. Either will do in the recipes in this book.

Sumac: My favorite ingredient. A Middle Eastern and Eastern Mediterranean spice ground from the sumac berry, it has a citrus flavor and was used when lemons were not in season. Use in salad dressings, rubs, and marinades. Available in spice shops and Mediterranean markets.

Tamari: A soy-based sauce, but not as salty as soy sauce and with a sweeter taste. It is good for salad dressings and dipping sauces, and in marinades, stews, and soups.

Thai red curry paste: A paste made from dried Thai red chiles, shallots, cilantro root, galangal, lemon grass, shrimp paste, fish sauce, kaffir lime leaves, and various dried spices. Keep a few jars on hand for use in stir-fries, coconut-based curries, and soups.

Toasted sesame oil: Asian sesame oil gets its characteristic flavor and dark color from the toasted sesame seeds. It has a nutty aromatic fragrance with a strong sesame taste. A little goes a long way.

index

metric conversions

Points to remember:

• A metric pint is equivalent to 600 mL (20 fluid ounces)

• An American pint (or 2 cups) is equivalent to 500 mL (16 fluid ounces)

• The standard US measuring cup is equivalent to 250 mL

• An American teaspoon is similar to a metric teaspoon (5 mL)

• An American tablespoon is slightly smaller than the metric tablespoon

Liquids

USA	Metric
1 $^1/_4$ tbsp	1 tbsp (15 mL)
2 $^1/_2$ tbsp	2 tbsp (30 mL)
$^1/_4$ cup	60 mL
$^1/_3$ cup	75 mL
$^1/_2$ cup	125 mL
$^2/_3$ cup	150 mL ($^1/_4$ pint)
1 cup ($^1/_2$ pint)	250 mL
1 $^1/_4$ cups	300 mL ($^1/_2$ pint)
1 $^1/_2$ cups	375 mL
1 $^3/_4$ cups	450 mL ($^3/_4$ pint)
1 pint (2 cups)	500 mL
2 $^1/_2$ cups	600 mL (1 pint)
4 cups (1 quart)	825 mL
4 $^1/_2$ cups	1 L
4 $^3/_4$ cups	1.2 L (2 pints)

Weights

USA	Metric
$^1/_2$ ounce	15 g
1 ounce	25 g
2 ounces	50 g
3 ounces	75 g
4 ounces ($^1/_4$ pound)	115 g
8 ounces ($^1/_2$ pound)	225 g
12 ounces ($^3/_4$ pound)	350 g
1 pound	500 g
1 $^1/_4$ pounds	675 g
1 $^3/_4$ pounds	750 g
2 pounds	1000 g/1 kg

Solid Fats

USA	Metric
1 tablespoon	15 g
2 tablespoons (1 ounce / $^1/_4$ stick)	25 g
4 tablespoons (2 ounces / $^1/_2$ stick)	50 g
8 tablespoons (4 ounces / 1 stick)	115 g
16 tablespoons (8 ounces / 2 sticks)	225 g

Flour

USA	Metric
2 tablespoons	15 g
$\frac{1}{2}$ cup	25 g
1 cup	115 g

Sugar

USA	Metric
2 tablespoons	25 g
$\frac{1}{2}$ cup	115 g
1 cup	225 g

Linear measurements

USA	Metric
$\frac{1}{4}$ inch	1 cm
$\frac{1}{2}$ inch	1.5 cm
$\frac{3}{4}$ inch	2 cm
1 inch	2.5 cm
4 inches	10 cm
6 inches	15 cm
7 inches	18 cm
8 inches	20 cm
9 inches	22.5 cm
10 inches	25 cm
11 inches	27.5 cm
12 inches	30 cm

Heat temperatures

Fahrenheit	Celsius
0°F (freezing)	-18°C
32°F	0°C
64°F	18°C
100°F	38°C
200°F	95°C
250°F	120°C
300°F	150°C
325°F	160°C
350°F	180°C
375°F	190°C
400°F	200°C
425°F	220°C
450°F	230°C
475°F	250°C
500°F	260°C